White Saviorism in International Development

Theories, Practices and Lived Experiences

Edited by

Themrise Khan
Kanakulya Dickson
Maïka Sondarjee

Daraja Press

2023

Published by Daraja Press
https://darajapress.com
Wakefield, Québec, Canada

Cover design: Hikmatullah Kharoti
Photo: Zach Vessels

In addition to minor corrections of the text, the cover image has been slightly modified for this second print run.

Library and Archives Canada Cataloguing in Publication

Title: White saviorism in international development : theories, practices and lived experiences /   edited by Themrise Khan, Kanakulya Dickson, Maïka Sondarjee.
Names: Khan, Themrise, editor. | Dickson, Kanakulya, editor. | Sondarjee, Maïka, editor.
Description: Includes bibliographical references.
Identifiers: Canadiana 20210187255 | ISBN 9781990263187 (softcover)
Subjects: LCSH: White people–Developing countries. | LCSH: White people –Psychology. | LCSH:
  Privilege (Social psychology)–Developing countries. | LCSH: Voluntarism –Developing countries. |
  LCSH: Economic assistance–Developing countries. | LCSH: Economic development–Developing
  countries.
Classification: LCC HT1575 .W55 2023 | DDC 305.809–dc23

Ivan Illich once said that "the road to hell is paved with good intentions." Very few books are willing to express this sentiment without hesitation. *White Saviorism in International Development* unveils the hypocrisies undergirding development projects led by the Global North for the Global South. It examines the intimate linkages between coloniality, development, and White Saviorism. The reader will quickly learn that White Saviorism is not only expressed at the individual level but, more importantly, is articulated at the institutional and structural levels. Everyone interested in interrogating the machinations of international financial institutions and non-governmental organizations and their central role in upholding the master narratives and practices of racial capitalism, colonialism, and heteropatriarchy should read this book. – **Jairo I. Fúnez-Flores**, Texas Tech University

White Saviorism in International Development is an important and timely book that should be read by all international development students and practitioners. It isn't easy reading, nor should it be, as it lays bare the deep flaws in the dominant international development system that has remained unchanged for over seven decades. The scope is admirably broad, from the history of White Saviorism to the lived experience of activists and practitioners worldwide. At a time when so much soul-searching is taking place across the sector, this book is an indispensable contribution to what many of us hope will be a new era in international cooperation. – **Dylan Mathews**, CEO Peace Direct, Chairperson CIVICUS Alliance

The is a terrific work of deep unmasking and engagement with the proverbial but always invisible elephant in the room of international development--that of the White gaze--correctly rendered here as "industrial-colonial-patriarchal-White savior complex"--indeed a problematic variant of the "God-complex." What is delivered here are multiple-faceted dimensions of the White gaze, including civilizational feminism. I have nothing but praise for this overdue work, whose shelf-life is guaranteed. Criticality is enhanced by elegance. – **Sabelo J. Ndlovu-Gatsheni,** Chair of Epistemologies of the Global South, University of Bayreuth, Germany

White Saviorism in International Development provides a model for critical collective writing. Combining praxis-informed theorization and accounts grounded in authors' own experiences in the White Savior Industrial Complex, these succinct and accessible chapters bring the realities of racial capitalism in international development to life. I was both educated and enraged! – **Alana Lentin,** author of *Why Race Still Matters*

This is a must-read book for anyone who wants to understand how many people contribute to upholding an oppressive White supremacist global system. There are libraries full of books and papers theorizing about and 'researching' those othered as 'under-developed' by colonial era discourses. These permeate the 'international development' and 'humanitarian' sectors today. They uphold the status quo - and it is time to dismantle them. In this intervention, the authors - all from the global majority and spanning over ten countries - turn the tables. They shine the light back at those discourses and agents perpetrating White Saviorism. This is "their voice, on their terms". There is much to learn from this collection, not least for those in the international 'development' and 'humanitarian' sectors. To not read it and engage with such critical scholarship and lived experiences would be a willful act of ignorance; of White supremacy." – **Amiera Sawas**, Researcher and Advocate

Table of contents

Foreword   vii
Olivia Alaso with Wendy Namatovu

Introduction: Why White Saviorism?   1
Kanakulya Dickson, Themrise Khan & Maïka Sondarjee

PART I: THEORY AND PRACTICE

1   Indigenous Cultures and the Industrial-Colonial-Patriarchal   27
White Savior Complex
Marcelo Saavedra-Vargas

2   Evaluation and the White Gaze in International Development   42
Sadaf Shallwani and Shama Dossa

3   The Warrior Logic of the White Savior   64
Leila Benhadjoudja

4   The Matriarchy Complex: White Feminist Disruption in   81
Development
Themrise Khan

5   False Consciousness and the Phenomenology of White   100
Saviorism
Kanakulya Dickson

6   Epistemological Underpinnings and Emancipatory Insights on   118
White Saviorism in Development
Kizito Michael George

7   Imposition and Reproduction of White Saviorism in Haiti   132
Rose Esther Sincimat Fleurant

8   The White Saviorism, Corporate Sector and Land Rights in   144
    Central Uganda
    Robert Kakuru

PART II: LIVED EXPERIENCES

9   White Saviorism, Green Colonialism and Sea Shepherd   162
    Fernando David Márquez Duarte

10 Today as Yesterday, the 'Savior Complex' of Europeans   169
    Anonymous 1

11 SUVs, Hotels and Faith: Experiences of White Privilege   176
    Amjad Mohamed Saleem

12 Macaulayputras and the 'Brown Saviors' in the World Bank's   184
    Advisory Services: A Story
    Anonymous 2

13 'H' is for Heroes With Hologram Haloes: A Testimony of   194
    Saviorism and Ministry
    Chongo Beverly Anne Mwila

14 The 'Local' and White Saviorism in the Caribbean   201
    Jody-Ann Anderson

15 Protecting Daughters for Gender 'Empowerment'   212
    Radha Shah

16 The White Savior Complex in International Cooperation   223
    Initiation Mandates
    Eddy Michel Yao

PART III: CONCLUSION

17 The Common Threads of White Saviorism   232
    Themrise Khan and Maïka Sondarjee

APPENDIX

About the Contributors   246

Foreword

Olivia Alaso with Wendy Namatovu[1]

As Teju Cole, a Nigerian-American writer and photographer, shared in a series of tweets back on 8 March 2012; 'From [Jeffrey] Sachs to [Nicholas] Kristof to Invisible Children to TED, the fastest growing industry in the USA is the White Savior Industrial Complex. The White Savior supports brutal policies in the morning, founds charities in the afternoon and receives awards in the evening'.

It is 2023, and nothing has changed.

The White Savior Industrial Complex is an outcome of racial capitalism. Like many other industrial complexes, White Saviorism, when interwoven within aid / charity / development work, deviates from any efforts aimed at actualizing justice to creating racialized profit economies. With race and capitalism as a constant factor, White Saviorism is built on the assumption that it is mainly individuals racialized as White who 'can make a difference' within Black and Brown communities.

While elevating White people is the norm, Black and Brown people too can exhibit White Savior tendencies depending on their position within the hierarchy of privileges. We have seen Ugandans, mainly those in positions of power, tap into the White Savior Complex. Politicians and celebrities sharing

---

[1] Olivia Alaso is a Co-Founder of *No White Saviors* and Anti-racist Activist, Wendy Namatovu is a member, *No White Saviors*

'oops' photos of themselves handing out donations were prevalent when COVID-19 cases were rising. Theoretically, we witnessed the White Savior Complex play out while I (Olivia) was pursuing my bachelor's degree in ethics and human rights at Makerere University in Kampala. There was a hyper-focus on alienating African and Black perspectives on human rights. If anything, African theories on human rights were rarely taught. The Black African's role within the human rights realm was to be protected, thought of, and for, constantly portrayed as lacking agency. This mentality and thought pattern linger within human rights practices and activism. In 2020, Ugandan climate activist Vanessa Nakate was cropped out of a photo taken at the World Economic Forum, Davos, Switzerland, where she appeared with other White climate activists. This action appears trivial but is an act of racism and White Saviorism: Vanessa's presence in the photo does not fit the narrative of 'predominantly White people championing environmental activism'.

White Saviorism is a symptom of racism and White supremacy, which reduces problems faced by mainly Black, Brown and Indigenous communities as easily solvable compared to those of predominantly White communities. White Saviorism does not prioritize impact but rather intentions. This is because, if anything, White Saviorism has always disguised itself as a kind-hearted, altruistic effort to solve 'development' problems of Black, Brown and Indigenous communities. The issue with this is that the same people who have invaded, colonized and exploited are the ones professing a commitment to solving the very problems they created in the first place.

White Saviorism is deeper than just a problematic selfie. While all forms of White Saviorism are rooted in the same unequal power dynamics, more extreme forms have resulted in severe trauma and even death. For instance, in the Renee Bach case in Uganda–an American woman, who at the age of 20, a mere high school graduate, ran an unregistered medical facility in Uganda, Jinja, with no medical training, and over 105 children eventually died in her facility. How could a 20-year-old American without medical training even think about running a medical facility in a foreign country? The reason? To be White is to be considered an expert, qualified and believed beyond a reasonable doubt in the global system of White supremacy. Especially when situated in Black and Brown spaces. The Renee Bach case is only the tip of the iceberg. Too much damage has been done in the name of good intentions in Black and Brown communities.

So how can individuals in positions of privilege, especially those racialized as White do better? How can we work within Black and Brown communities without perpetuating the White Savior Complex? One word: Listen.

We cannot stress how much we hate the concept of any community being 'voiceless'. Individuals in positions of privilege have an incredible opportunity to give space and a platform to the voices of people working within their communities to meet the critical needs that they are passionate about. Renee Bach could have worked with a local hospital within Jinja by extending financial assistance, but instead chose otherwise to center herself and not the community she claimed to help.

If we want any real ethical, sustainable change tangibly, we must consider how race and capitalism intersect to create oppressive systems. The development sector needs to move away from charity to actualizing justice. Predominantly White countries, institutions and people need to work with, not for Black / Brown / Indigenous communities. Peoples of the 'Global South' need not be 'othered'. It is vital for organizations founded in predominantly White countries to know that they are not 'experts' and cannot effectively solve problems impacting communities that have been over-exploited.

Due to the insidious nature of White Saviorism, there has been little or no research done. International development is and has been the pivot of White Saviorism, allowing it to spread like cancer. From research to practice, the sector has created a false abode that justifies the continuous intervention of predominantly White institutions–from Eurocentric institutional policies like the structural adjustment programs of the IMF to big INGOs that hire mostly individuals racialized as White as country heads to White 'experts' who want to fix Black and Brown problems–all this while maintaining the status quo and justifying the narrative that the African continent needs 'saving'.

This book answers many pre-existing questions about White Saviorism and asks new ones. Most importantly, this book offers insights into why as Black women, we will not take part in respectability politics or color-blind racism. It poses very crucial yet uncomfortable questions to those racialized as White / including White allies / co-conspirators who proclaim a commitment to racial and social justice. From the proselytizer White Savior seeking to convert people to the Christian faith to the cultural White Savior on the journey to spread 'superior White' cultural ways to the ideational White Savior, this book is for them. From the American White woman feminist who believes teaching Afghan girls how to skateboard will save' them to the White feminist fronting the campaign to 'end' female genital mutilation in Africa, this book is for those and others that look like us and who have internalized their false inferior status as deserving, for those racialized as Black and are struggling with anti-Blackness. I hope this book guides you on ethically working with communities that are not your own without centering some preconceived notions of White supremacy. This book is a foundational pillar for those embarking on a decolonial journey.

Kampala, Uganda,
Fall 2022

Introduction:
Why White Saviorism?

Kanakulya Dickson, Themrise Khan
and Maïka Sondarjee

W estern practitioners and scholars often establish that development as a field of study and a geopolitical project started in the 1940s, with the establishment of the International Bank for Reconstruction and Development (now the World Bank). American President Harry Truman, in his 1947 inaugural address, reinforced the narrative behind the Western enterprise of development assistance to previously colonized countries, which defined what it meant to be 'developed' versus 'underdeveloped'. Since then, in addition to multilateral organizations and bilateral donors, non-governmental organizations and civil society organizations have devoted an increasing number of resources to address global inequalities and poverty in all its forms. As a result, official development assistance amounted to an all-time high in 2021, up to $178.9 billion, an increase of 4.4 percent from 2020 (in real terms) (OECD 2021.

The racial hierarchy developed during colonization, where some countries are / aren't modern and civilized, became the historical root of the development ladder determining which countries are / are not developed (Parpart 1995). Mies and Shiva (1993) have argued that the need to 'civilize' African populations during colonization slowly transformed into the

1

need to 'develop' them (Crush 1995, Kothari 2006, Pieterse and Parekh 1995). Once the colonial enterprise vanished after cycles of decolonial fights, Africans, Latin Americans and Asians were no longer 'uncivilized' but 'underdeveloped' which became 'in development', or for the luckiest ones, 'emergent' (Manji and O'Coill 2002, p. 7). The emergence of teleological imaginary, not unlike the colonizers' one from Barbary to civilization, assumes that there is a potential progressive movement from 'underdeveloped', to 'in development', to 'emergent', to 'developed', a movement 'from badness to goodness' (Shanin 1997, p. 65). The colonial vernaculars of 'barbarians' or 'animals' have been replaced with 'ethnicity', 'underdeveloped' or 'traditional societies', terms which are less obviously dehumanizing but are still 'imbued with narratives of othering, backwardness or exoticization' (Kagal and Latchford 2020, p. 22).

Thus, in the aftermath of independence movements, Western organizations reinforced this vision of the field, which rebranded colonial relationships as 'development' ones, where the Global North continues to see Global South communities and governments through the prism of inferiority. The colonial idea that the Global South is a series of lacks still undergirds the development field (Goudge 2003, Grovogui 2001, Tamale 2020). In short, it is full of places of 'suffering, starvation and bloodshed' (Pieterse 1992, p. 235).

This narrative leads to a paradox in the relationship between the Global South and the Global North. If the capitalist system encourages unequal trade relationships to favor profits over common goods, well-intentioned Western individuals and organizations devise and implement projects to 'develop' Black and Brown communities worldwide. Walter Rodney captured this view in his classical work, *How Europe Underdeveloped Africa* (1973), where he explains how

European economic practices after colonization ended up curtailing Africa's potential economic progress. In his view, the Europeans extracted natural resources for exportation to the Global North, making the colonial metropoles rich, meanwhile creating economic misery for the colonized territories. The intention of Global North individuals and organizations to 'save' communities in Global South countries often comes with a lack of acknowledgment of their role in the establishment and the perpetuation of inequalities, namely through colonization, capitalist practices of exploitation of Global South workers, dispossession of Indigenous communities and devaluation of women from the Global South.

Calling countries 'underdeveloped' or 'in development' while they have been systematically exploited, dispossessed and oppressed within colonization, then capitalism, is ironic. This racial hierarchy or coloniality of power (Fanon 1961, Quijano 2007), through which historically colonized countries and people are considered as having fewer capabilities, coupled with the impression of benevolence and altruism of Western agents, is what we call White Saviorism. Western development practitioners often act on pretences of generosity and goodwill, and the whole development industry is based on Whiteness as the norm of progress, modernity and development. As the preface to this volume states, White Saviorism is not only about individually held attitudes, it is about a system of White supremacy and power. As Rose Esther S. F. argues in her contribution, if colonialism and slavery in underdeveloped countries like Haiti, White Saviorism supports a continued subalternization and theft of its resources.

This Introduction paints the paradox of how White development practitioners want to 'save' racialized communities while supporting a capitalist system that encourages land grabs, exploitation of Black and Brown bodies and dispossession of local knowledge and worldviews. This collective volume thus underlines the development field's racist tendencies, colonial attitudes, lack of accountability, hypocrisy, lack of respect for communities in the Global South, lack of inclusion and its overall support for a capitalist system of exploitation and dispossession. This state of the field, we argue, is due to a structure of White Saviorism. Why are people from the Global South still under-considered and marginalized in global discussions about world development? All underpinned by the archaic notion that only White people can 'save' the others.

WHAT IS WHITE SAVIORISM?

The editors of this book define White Saviorism as an (often ignored) overarching structure in the field of international development. It is simultaneously a state of mind and a concrete unequal power structure between the Global North and the Global South. White Saviorism is founded on the benevolence of Whiteness, which elevates people of White European descent despite their role in exploiting and dispossessing people from the Global South. Their self-perception as more capable, more intelligent and thus more 'developed' directs their actions in communities of the Global South. The helping imperative often comes in contradiction with a system of capitalist exploitation and dispossession.

In short, White Saviorism is a structure of racial hierarchy that not only strips the agency of racialized people but also falsely implies that White agents need to save them from their positions as victims. In the context of international development, this structure is visible in aid campaigns, sporadic or recurrent development initiatives, international organizations' practices and social media posts. It is often translated in day-to-day practices in a condescending posture based on the primacy and the superiority of Whiteness. White Saviorism is also about the hierarchies on which the development industry rests. It includes mentalities (individual), narratives (cultural) and the White Savior Industrial Complex (institutional and systemic) (Willer-Kherbaoui 2019, p. 10).

Other definitions of White Saviorism, also known as the 'White Savior Complex (White Savior Complex)' or 'syndrome', include 'the phenomenon in which a White person "guides" people of color from the margins to the mainstream with his or her initiative and benevolence, which tends to render the people of color "incapable of helping themselves" and disposes them of historical agency' (Cammarota 2011, n.d., Willuweit 2020). This definition points to an interesting tendency of White people to perceive themselves as able to guide people of color and refers to the dispossession of the agency of people of color. It captures an essential aspect of the White Savior attitude as a self-appointed task and the assumption of knowing best. It believes that it is the White individual's responsibility to save people of color because they lack the willpower and intelligence to do so themselves.

A significant aspect of White Saviorism is a 'sense of obligation', a 'helping imperative' (Heron 2007, p. 26). Flaherty (2016, p. 13) calls this the savior mentality, the idea that a deus ex machina or 'a hero' will arrive and answer someone else's societal problems. Even the worst massacres, Flaherty explains, are often portrayed as a way for 'virtuous men' to save women and children (Benhadjoudja, this volume). White / Western actors, or those perpetuating racial hierarchies, have a persistent feeling that not only 'can' they do something, but they 'need' to do something about Global South poverty. While there is a clear need for greater

5

international solidarity to face global challenges like pandemics or the climate crisis, this paternalistic mindset of helping / charity rather than fighting injustices can be detrimental in the long term (Edwards 2006, Sondarjee 2020). This sense of obligation refers to what Rudyard Kipling unironically called 'The White Man's Burden' in his 1899 poem, where he framed a call for help to the unfortunate Black people: 'Take up the White Man's burden [...] Fill full the mouth of Famine. And bid the sickness cease'.

For example, the 2020 WE Charity scandal in Canada disclosed more than collusion in the attribution of federal funds. The WE Charity was a Canadian organization founded by Craig and Marc Kielburger and known for 'voluntourism', celebrity spokespeople and concert-style youth rallies, all supposedly for the benefit of the Global South. It was later found that international volunteers were accomplishing basic tasks like repainting walls or moving bricks from one site to another, which, according to various observers, could have easily been replaced or better served by the local workforce (Klaassen 2020, Jefferess 2020). Ultimately, the Kielburger brothers not only violated financial guidelines, but many of their international projects did not even exist.

Trying to capture the multifaceted nature beyond the savior 'mentality', Teju Cole coined the term 'White Savior Industrial Complex', to point at a more extensive web of intricate North / South relations rather than a few bad apples in the development ecosystem. Mentioning American-backed coups, American militarization and Western interests in Africa, he qualifies the White Savior Industrial Complex as 'a valve for releasing the unbearable pressures that build in a system built on pillage' (Cole 2012). The 'missionaries of development' represent a system inherited from colonialism and supported by individuals with good intentions who have no intention of modifying the North / South mechanisms of exploitation (Manji and O'Coill 2002, Sondarjee 2020). Cole endeavors to capture the various aspects of White Saviorism, and by combining the two adjectives 'industrial' and 'complex', he reveals the dissociative nature of White Saviorism, which harms people of color and yet pretends to save them. He adds that we can participate in the 'economic destruction' of countries like Haiti over time but 'when the earthquake strikes, it feels good to send $10 each to the rescue fund'. One of the tweets that led to the writing of Cole's groundbreaking article in The Atlantic sums it up: 'The White Savior Industrial Complex is not about justice. It is about having a big emotional experience that validates privilege' (Cole 2012).

Cole was specifically addressing the 2012 campaign #Kony2012, led by the American organization Invisible Children and its founder, the American Jason Russell, which became emblematic of a self-centered endeavor. 'Everything in my heart told me to do something' (7:30) is one of the symbolic quotes of their flagship short documentary and social media campaign on Joseph Kony, then #1 war criminal according to the International Criminal Court. The impulse behind the movie was that Western populations did not know about the warlord, and if only they knew, then the conflict would resolve itself. After showing Russell's quest to help his Ugandan friend Jacob overcome hardships, one of the most cathartic moments of the promotional video is when a group of White people says 'We've seen these kids. We've heard their cries. This war must end. [...] We will fight war' (16:45).

However, we believe that adding the adjectives 'complex' or 'syndrome' in defining White Saviors sometimes limits its scope as an unconscious psychological condition or a symptom of another ailment. But as investigations and testimonies in this book indicate, White Saviorism is complicated, multifaceted and systemic. And while it ends up alleviating poverty on the margins, it undermines the 'the struggle[s] of [Global South] people to emancipate themselves from economic, social and political oppression' and often reinforces the capitalist-heteropatriarchal system (Manji and O'Coill 2002, p. 568; Sondarjee 2020). Moreover, the systemic character of White Saviorism goes beyond individual attitudes and actions to include structures of aid and development practices. Therefore, in this volume, we choose the word White Saviorism rather than 'White Savior Complex' or 'White Savior Syndrome' to emphasize the character as a racial structure of power rather than an individually held attitude.

The systemic aspect of White Saviorism is visible in two ways. First, individual 'benevolent' development practices often support a capitalist, colonial, heteronormative and gendered world system. Foundations like the ones supported by Bill and Melinda Gates will implement projects, while trying to maximize profits at the expense of workers in the Gates companies. Or else, while a Canadian project can aim at 'empowering' women in Guatemala, the Canadian government simultaneously refuses to acknowledge the harsh conditions of seasonal migrants from Guatemala, the impact of trade agreements between the two countries or of the hundreds of women from Guatemala doing housework in Canada. While trying to empower women from the Global South with its Feminist International Assistance Policy, the Canadian or the French government also simultaneously adopts laws that restrict the rights of women wearing the hijab in their country and allow for an increase of gendered violence against them.

The second systemic aspect of White Saviorism refers to global colonial racial hierarchies. The problem is that American missionaries without medical training think they are superior to African doctors and that the development ladder devalues the humanness and capacities of racialized populations in the Global South. The problem is not that Jason Russell wants to help capture Joseph Kony. The problem is that despite being 'considerate' and 'ethical' (Stake 2004, p. 103) and 'committed, passionate human beings' (Arcaro 2016, p. xi), development organizations create narratives supported by colonial hierarchies that perpetuate overall unequal systems. Narratives create material and institutionalized prejudice. By participating in White Saviorism, well-intentioned development workers are placed in positions of power because of their race and perceived White supremacy (Goudge 2003). Not because of their actual capabilities and expertise. These narratives promote an alterity process between us and them and reinforce the idea that we can solve their problems (Escobar 1995). It creates the false narrative that the development industry is not about fighting injustice but about civilizing the 'underdeveloped', the 'barbarians' (Manji and O'Coill 2002, Sondarjee 2020).

TYPOLOGY OF WHITE SAVIORISM

The literature defines six different types of White Saviors:

Proselytizer White Savior: The proselytizer seeks to convert people to the Christian faith. The proselytizing White Savior has been made to believe that she has a better faith system, which grants them a right to change those in the Global South (see Etherington 1983, Johnston 1887, Nunn 2010). This was historically reflected in religious missionary work and is also rooted in the historical-theological tradition that apportioned the personhood of a 'savior' to the White person, White Savior or European.

Cultural White Savior: This is the White Savior who has apportioned itself the mission of spreading White cultural ways. This category broadly falls under those who believe that the White race has a superior culture and, therefore divine duty to civilize other peoples who are savages and backward culturally. Brantlinger (1985) exhaustively proved that Victorian England designated Africa a 'dark continent'; at the same time, a pseudo-sociological science referred to as 'orientalism' emerged as a strategy of power and subjugation.

Sojourner White Savior: Sojourner means the traveler or wanderer who moves from place to place to 'develop' those who are 'underdeveloped'. This kind of White Savior is a brave traveler who moves from their home in the Global North and settles among the needy and unworthy people in distant lands to do humanitarian work or development projects. This has given rise to the 'volunteerism industry' or the 'charity industry', which has done some commendable good, but with a far-reaching negative impact on the agency of the needy to work themselves out of need (Driessens *et al.*, 2012, Lupton 2011).

Remainer White Savior: This savior remains back at home and sends donations to good causes of charity. These are the ones who donate their widow's mite, however poor they may be, in the service of 'saving' other humans elsewhere. Their altruism can be both genuine and based on a kind of magical thinking. This type of White Saviorism funds the many charities and CSOs operating around the world that fuel the global White Savior Industrial Complex.

Ideational White Savior: This variety of White Saviorism refers to those who think they have a divine duty to come up with superior ideas and theories for the benefit of needy people worldwide. These may come in the form of scholars, researchers or even diplomats with better ideas for the good of humanity. They write articles and books and generate development theories that are considered superior to the Global South. They often rely on research assistants from the countries they study, who have greater knowledge of the languages and the local specificities.

Baird (2021) observed that before the 17th century, Europeans had no self-perception of belonging to a White race, 'but once the idea was invented, it quickly began to reshape the modern world'. The colonial narrative leads to an assumption that

Whiteness is 'the primary referent of power, prestige and progress across the world' (Pailey 2020, p. 733). Whiteness was created as a racial hierarchy of agency, epistemic capabilities and humanness (Ndlovu-Gatsheni 2018, Tamale 2020). Development scholars and practitioners view their work through this gaze: 'The "White gaze" of development measures the political, socio-economic and cultural processes of Southern Black, Brown and other people of color against a standard of Northern Whiteness and finds them incomplete, wanting, inferior or regressive. In essence, White is always right, and West is always best' (Pailey 2020, p. 733).

During colonial rule, the colonial masters labored to transform territories under their control into economically profitable colonial projects, eventually entrenched with capitalist production and profit-making practices. This effort has informed development practice as we know it today in much of the Global South. Almost all former colonies perennially score poor development indicators both in human and economic terms but participate in enriching the global elite of the world. The perception of the colonized peoples as evolutionary inferior to the colonial masters infected the financial practices in these territories, resulting in viewing them as basic resources for exploitation (Manji and O'Coill 2002, Sondarjee 2020). Even religious crusaders justified massacres under saviorism pretenses to save people from the 'wicked race' (Flaherty 2016, p. 14). Similarly, Christopher Columbus justified the genocide of the Americas to save the soul of non-Christians.

Despite some justification for the colonial project, the established colonial systems made it evident from the beginning that the British were interested in colonial territories for economic expediency and not for the civilization of the native Africans. The machinations of the colonial state were to facilitate the economic benefit of the masters. From 1887 when Sir Mackinnon formed the British East Africa Association, which finally transformed into the Imperial British East Africa Company, the expectation was to facilitate the exploitation of native labor, extraction of natural resources and export of minerals. When Mackinnon's business venture ran bankrupt due to extensive uprisings and a long civil war in Buganda in 1892, the British government took over direct control of the colony to ensure the continuous exploitation of resources. Therefore, the idea of 'benign imperialism' which stated that the purpose was not to 'seize land, labor and commodities but to teach the natives English, table manners and double-entry book-keeping' is a myth (Monbiot 2012).

The idea of benign imperialism has the same roots as the savior mentality of many development workers in the modern era. Apparently, the purpose was not to 'seize land, labour and commodities but to teach the natives English, table manners and double-entry book-keeping' (Monbiot 2012). The continued exploitation of colonized territories is wrapped in a manufactured falsehood that suffers a lack when scrutinized closely. This background provides the context and container within which the discussions in this book emanate; the unifying question that the different strands of views presented in the different chapters is whether contemporary development practices and charity work propagated in the Global South succeeded in extrapolating them from their original biased colonial background.

Terms like capacity-building, technical expert, consultant and expatriate, often used in the sector, are infused with a colonial hierarchy. For example, the term expatriate does not apply to a South African in Canada nor to a Haitian in France, but to Western agents in the Global South. The term capacity-building is probably the most potent in its assumptions of

White superiority: 'The concept of capacity building (and its ideologies and practices) is effective and potent because it is cast as technical and rational. Yet, in its mesmerizing repetitions, capacity building also depends on the ideological and political construction of the incapacity of African countries–that is, cultural, developmental and civilizational lack' (Kothari 2006, p. 15, Pierre 2020, p. 93). This is not just a belief but refers to the colonial hierarchical structure of knowledge production: 'The message is that they are the experts in all things has been reinforced since birth. They are taught that saving others is the burden they must bear' (Flaherty 2016). Far from being an imposition by White agents on non-White ones, this mindset can also be seen when aid-receiving populations attribute higher status to external White consultants rather than 'one of their own' (Wilson 2012).

WHITE SAVIORISM IN PRACTICE

With the global reckoning of racism in the international development sector, particularly since the murder of George Floyd by American law enforcement in 2020, White development workers can no longer ignore how they contribute to the 'institutionalized world order' (Sondarjee 2020). Many of the theoretical concepts outlined in this Introduction and documented in the various contributions are rooted in many recent and real examples of how damaging White Saviorism has been to the non-European, non-White world, not necessarily in terms of how the former treats the latter, but within the structures of these organizations themselves.

Some of the most prominent examples have been in traditionally savior-oriented development agencies. Oxfam expatriate staff, for instance, were accused of sexual exploitation of women in Haiti during the 2010 earthquake relief efforts. (Gayle 2018). Yet another investigation revealed sexual abuse and sex for money allegations by local women against international aid workers from the World Health Organizations, Médecins sans Frontières, Oxfam, World Vision and UNICEF in the Democratic Republic of Congo during the Ebola crisis between 2018 and 2020 (Flummerfelt 2020). White Saviorism enabled these workers to exploit women in the Global South with impunity.

A more recent scandal that broke out in 2022 was of the medical charity organization Médecins sans Frontières 'profiting from exploitative images'. It was found that MSF had been using images of child rape survivors without their consent to fundraise for their work. Graphic images of recently raped young women and others undergoing abortions were put up on sale online in stock image libraries at high costs. Not only is this an appalling ethical violation of privacy and human rights but an abhorrent example of the White Savior mentality ingrained among structures such as fundraising by White development organizations.

There are several examples in the international development industry, which are only the tip of the iceberg. The notion of White Saviorism and racist control goes beyond the relationships between the North and South. Members of the sector published several reports and surveys in the last few years identifying structural racism underpinning international aid organizations' internal staffing structures and behavior. They have ranged from definitions of racial equity within global development to the experiences of Black, Indigenous and other people of color (BIPOC) working in the sector to the British government's delayed sub-inquiry into racism in British aid. Volunteer coalitions such as Decolonize MSF, No White Saviors, Charity So White and the Racial Equality Index, among others, have systematically exposed the racist undertones of how the aid sector treats its own racialized staff, let alone how it treats its 'partners' in the Global South. The 'decolonization' of aid is now the rising mantra in the international development industry as it rushes to salvage its image as a ruthless, exploitative and racist undertaking.[1] Exposing such evidence should lead to some accountability on behalf of the development industry in coming to terms with its reality. However, accountability can only occur if members of the sector understand White Saviorism as a structural inequality within international development. Hopefully, this book will participate in this process.

WHY A COLLECTIVE BOOK ON WHITE SAVIORISM

From the outset, we, as instigators of this project, were clear that the contributions of this book would solely reflect voices from the Global South. White Saviorism cannot be viewed or understood from a White perspective–the perspective of saviors themselves. Therefore, our call for abstracts for this book made it clear that we would only welcome submissions from authors who belonged to the Global South or originated from it. Despite that, we still received submissions from White development practitioners who wanted to contribute with apologizing narratives. One submission even felt the need to critique Black and Brown people's behavior and attitudes as a reason they needed to be 'saved'. They thought that the 'insights' they built during their time as privileged White people in countries of the South needed to be heard because they 'understood' said countries better. The contributions in this volume are thus an attempt not only to define a concept of

---

[1] This book does not have the space to address the full decolonization discussion as part of un-packing White Saviorism.

White Saviorism but to develop more democratic research and publication practices.

For the book to resonate among a wide audience and reflect a broad cross-section of knowledge and experiences, we also consciously did not follow a purely academic route. White Saviorism is not an academic phenomenon *per se*, but an actual lived one, which all of us who interact with the powerful Global North experience daily. Therefore, we have attempted to bring together academic knowledge, practitioner-based approaches and personal stories of those who have experienced White Saviorism first-hand. In combination, these contributions highlight the historical, functional, operational and personal impacts of White Saviorism in a field prepositioned on the act of 'doing good'.

Throughout the development of this book, we did not wish to impose any sets of rules and expression guidelines on our authors. We intended to capture the broad range of historical and lived experiences and the authenticity of the author's feelings toward the subject. The contributions are meant to be their ideas and their voice on their terms. Therefore, we did not attempt to pressure authors to identify themselves. We understand that many of them took risks to share these accounts, and we respect the decision that some chose to remain anonymous. We also allowed authors to express themselves in any way they felt comfortable–from submitting fictionalized accounts of their experiences to submitting in a language of their preference to using a more stylized approach in their expression. It is this rich and varied mix that we feel brings out the true extent of the impact of White Saviorism.

We have tried to highlight as widely as possible a variety of regions of the Global South and issues based on our submissions, which show the negative impacts of White Saviorism on international development as both a profession and a line of thought. Given this, we have divided the book into two sections: theories and practices, which look at the historical impacts of colonialism and show how those who have been part of the international development sector in the Global South view its discourse and practices from the inside; and lived experiences, which are the raw, personal stories of those who have faced the brunt of White Saviorism in their work as development professionals from the Global South.

The first section begins by underlining the colonial history of White Saviorism coupled with the near extinction of Indigenous Peoples and cultures of North America by the White colonial explorers. Dr Marcelo Saavedra-Vargas, himself an Indigenous Elder, writes in Chapter 1 about how the land of Abya-Yala was decimated by the Spanish colonial conquistadors and the impact that still has on his people today. He explores the idea that some colonizers, like Bartolomé de las Casas, acted under the guise of White Saviorism.

In Chapter 2, Sadaf Shallwani and Shama Dossa continue this analysis of colonial Whiteness by combining theory and practice. They claim that evaluation in global development 'establishes Whiteness as the norm and demonstrates how interventions designed and funded by the Global North are necessary and effective–thereby reinforcing the "feel good" element of the White Saviorism'.

Chapter 3 highlights the intersectional aspects of the White Saviorism structure. Themrise Khan coins the term the 'Matriarchy Complex' in this chapter which focuses on the impact of White women in development (WID). She critiques the role of White Western WID who take on the condescending role of a matriarch over their Brown and Black counterparts in the South. In Chapter 4, Leila Benhadjoudja argues that modern-day imperial warfare has attempted to use Brown women as needing to be 'saved'. She studies the warrior logic of White Saviorism in the Afghan war against the Taliban, which was waged to strengthen the geopolitical position of the United States in the Middle East, under the guise of 'saving Afghan women'.

The next three contributors analyze the philosophical underpinnings of White Saviorism as visible in practices. Chapter 5 by Kanakulya Dickson develops a philosophical account to answer the fundamental questions of the ethical aspects of White Saviorism within the development industry. Michael George Kizito uses an unusual argument in Chapter 6 to frame how White Saviorism 'is actualized through the implicit and explicit inculcation of opinions, attitudes, perceptions, biases, distortions, disinformation and misinformation about development, poverty and well-being right from childhood to adulthood'. Robert Kakuru then illustrates in Chapter 7, through case studies, the irony that Western agents encourage land grabbing and then try to 'help' the Global South population impacted by land violations. To close this section, Rose Esther SF uses personal experiences in Chapter 8 to conceptualize White Saviorism in modern-day Haiti. She documents how colonialism, exploitation and Whiteness have manifested in the country.

The second section on lived experiences is an incredibly personal journey for many of our authors who were kind enough to share them with us. Some fictionalized, some in first-person, authors recount actual events that authors themselves experienced during their careers in international development. Chapters 9 and 10, respectively, build on the colonial aspects of White Saviorism developed in Section 1. In Chapter 9, Fernando David Márquez Duarte studies how environmental protection practices are built on a colonial mindset of 'we know best', destroying local livelihoods. Then, in Chapter 10, an anonymized author studies ethnotourism in the Democratic Republic of the Congo, a practice based on the colonial devaluation of Africans and the perceived benevolence of modern-day tourism.

The following two chapters add a layer of complexity to the understanding of White Saviorism developed in the last section by speaking of 'local' White Saviors. In Chapter 11, Amjad Mohamad Saleem recounts his time as the lone 'Brown' Muslim aid worker during the tsunami relief efforts in Sri Lanka. Another one of our contributors fictionalizes the notion of the 'Brown savior' in a story set in a World Bank office in Bangladesh in Chapter 12. These authors follow Shallwani and Dosa and the editors of this book by conceptualizing White Saviorism as a structure of Whiteness rather than the evil deeds of a few ill-intentioned White agents. Chapter 13, which echoes Benhadjoudja and Khan, highlights the gendered aspects of White Saviorism. Radha Shah tells her story here as a gender development consultant in Pakistan researching the local implementation of internationally funded projects who observed the adoption of White Saviorism narratives within a cultural elite savior complex.

The last three chapters then integrate theoretical insights into the recollection of lived experiences of White Saviorism. In Chapter 14, Jody-Ann Anderson narrates her perspective of a 'local' Programme Officer with an international NGO in the Caribbean. In Chapter 15, Chongo Beverly Anne Mwila narrates her experiences working at a White run charity for child sponsorship in Zambia called Heaven's Heroes, which was anything but given their dubious organizational behavior and treatment of staff. Finally, in Chapter 16, Eddy Michel Yao writes about his first experience in the world of international cooperation as a 23-year-old volunteer born in Côte d'Ivoire but raised in Canada.

We thank the editors and reviewers at Daraja Press, especially Firoze Manji, for his trust and indefectible support in this project. We also want to thank Hikmatullah Kharoti, from Afghanistan, for the brilliant cover design (photo by Zach Vessels). We believe that this book is extremely significant. To us, as editors, to everyone from the Global South, and in the field of international development, we hope reading these different accounts will lead to some realization of how the international development profession has consciously and unconsciously impeded progress in the Global South, not accelerated it. We also wish that this collection is only the first in many more that reflect on the stories of professionals and scholars of the Global South who the Global North has subjugated in their own countries. There needs to be a tectonic shift in how White Saviors have been conditioned by decades of colonialism to consider racialized people inferior. This reckoning will be a long and fluctuating process that we urgently need to embark on.

REFERENCES

Abu-Lughod, L. (2002) 'Do Muslim women really need saving? Anthropological reflections on cultural relativism and its others', *American Anthropologist*, 104(3): 783-90

African Union (2016) *Illicit Financial Flow: Report of the High-Level Panel on Illicit Financial Flows From Africa*, Addis Ababa, African Union

Arcaro, T. (2016) *Aid Worker Voices: Survey Results and Commentary, USA* (online), Createspace Independent Publishing Platform

Baird, R. (2021) 'The invention of Whiteness: The long history of a dangerous idea'. *The Guardian*, 20 April, https://www.theguardian.com/news/2021/apr/20/the-invention-of-Whiteness-long-history-dangerous-idea, accessed 5 December 2022

Bex, S. and Craps, S. (2016) 'Humanitarianism, testimony, and the White Savior industrial complex: What is the what versus Kony 2012', *Cultural Critique*, 92: 32-56

Brantlinger, P. (1985) 'Victorians and Africans: The genealogy of the myth of the Dark Continent', *Critical Inquiry*, vol. 12, no. 1:166-76

Brown, F. and Hall, D. (2008) 'Tourism and development in the Global South: The issues', *Third World Quarterly*, 29(5): 839-49

Bruce-Raeburn, A. (2019) 'International development has a race problem', *Devex*, 19 May, https://www.devex.com/news/opinion-international-development-has-a-race-problem-94840, accessed 5 December 2022

Cammarota, J. (2011) 'Blindsided by the Avatar: White Saviors and allies out of Hollywood and in education', *Review of Education, Pedagogy, and Cultural Studies*, vol. 33, no. 3:243-4

Cole, T. (2012) 'The White-Savior industrial complex', *The Atlantic*, 21 March, https://www.theatlantic.com/international/archive/2012/03/the-White-savior-industrial-complex/254843/, accessed 5 December 2022

Crush, J.S. (ed) (1995) *Power of Development*, London, New York, Routledge

Dickson, K (2020) 'Pan Africanism Part 1 w/Kanakulya Dickson', *No White Savior Podcast*, 9 March

Driessens, O., Stijn, J. and Daniel, B. (2012) 'The X-factor of charity: A critical analysis of celebrities' involvement in the 2010 Flemish and Dutch Haiti relief shows', *Media, Culture & Society*, vol. 34, no. 6:709-25

Easterly, W. (2006) *The White Man's Burden: Why the West's Efforts to Aid the Rest Have Done so Much Ill and so Little Good*, New York, Penguin Press

Edwards, V.M. (2006) 'Aspiring social justice ally identity development: A conceptual model', *NASPA Journal*, 43(4): 39-60

Escobar, A. (1995) *Encountering Development: The Making and Unmaking of the Third World*, Princeton, Princeton University Press

Etherington, N. (1983) 'Missionaries and the intellectual history of Africa: A historical survey', *Itinerario*, vol. 7, no. 2:116-43

Fanon, F. (1961) *Les Damnés de La Terre*, Paris, Maspéro

Flaherty, J. (2016) *No More Heroes. Grassroots Challenges to the Savior Mentality, Chico,* AK Press

Flummerfelt, R. (2020) 'EXCLUSIVE: More than 50 women accuse aid workers of sex abuse in Congo Ebola crisis', *The New Humanitarian*, 29 September, https://www.thenewhumanitarian.org/2020/09/29/exclusive-more-50-women-accuse-aid-workers-sex-abuse-congo-ebola-crisis, accessed 5 December 2022

Frye, M. (1992) 'White Woman Feminist', in Willful Virgin: *Essays in Feminism 1976-1992*, pp. 147-69, Freedom, The Crossing Press

Gayle, D. (2018) 'Timeline: Oxfam sexual exploitation scandal in Haiti', The Guardian, 15 June, https://www.theguardian.com/world/2018/jun/15/timeline-oxfam-sexual-exploitation-scandal-in-haiti, accessed 5 December 2022

Goudge, P. (2003) *The Power of Whiteness: Racism in Third World Development and Aid,* London, Lawrence & Wishart

Grovogui, S.N. (2001) 'Come to Africa: A hermeneutics of race in international theory', *Alternatives*, 26(4): 425-48

Heron, B. (2007) *Desire for Development: Whiteness, Gender, and the Helping Imperative*, Waterloo, Wilfrid Laurier University Press

hooks, b. (2001) *Ain't I a Woman: Black Women and Feminism,* Pluto Classics, London, Pluto Press

Hughey, M.W. (2014) 'The savior trope and the modern meanings of Whiteness', in *The White Savior Film: Content, Critics, and Consumption*, Philadelphia, Temple University Press

Jefferess, D. (2020) 'WE charity and the White Savior Complex', *Canadian Dimension*, 12 August, https://canadiandimension.com/articles/view/we-charity-and-the-White-Savior-complex, accessed 5 December 2022

Johnston, H.H. (1887) 'British missions and missionaries in Africa', *The Nineteenth Century: A Monthly Review,* (129): 708-24

Kagal, N. and Latchford , L. (2020) 'Towards an intersectional praxis in international development: What can the sector learn from Black feminists located in the Global North?', *Gender & Development*, 28(1): 11-30

Kagumire, R. (2012) 'Kony2012; my response to invisible children's campaign', *African Feminisms, Gender, Human Rights, Peace and*

Conflict (blog), 8 March, https://rosebellkagumire.com/2012/03/08/kony2012-my-response-to-invisible-childrens-campaign/, accessed 5 December 2022

Khan, T. (2021) 'Racism doesn't just exist within aid. It's the structure the sector is built on', *The Guardian,* 31 August, https://www.theguardian.com/global-development/2021/aug/31/racism-doesnt-just-exist-within-aid-its-the-structure-the-sector-is-built-on, accessed 5 December 2022

Klaassen, R. (2020) 'We really need to talk about WE's White Savior complex', *Huffington Post,* 15 July, https://www.huffpost.com/archive/ca/entry/we-charity-volunteer-White-Savior_ca_5f0e0652c5b648c301f07314, accessed 5 December 2022

Kothari, U. (2006) 'An agenda for thinking about "race" in development', *Progress in Development Studies,* 6(1): 9-23

Levy, A. (2020) 'A missionary on trial', *The New Yorker,* 13 April, https://www.newyorker.com/magazine/2020/04/13/a-missionary-on-trial, accessed 5 December 2022

Lough, B.J. and Carter-Black, J. (2015) 'Confronting the White elephant: International volunteering and racial (dis)advantage', *Progress in Development Studies,* 15(3): 207-20

Lupton, D.R. (2011) *Toxic Charity: How the Church Hurts Those They Help and How to Reverse It,* New York, HarperCollins Publishers

Manji, F. and O'Coill, C. (2002) 'The missionary position: NGOs and development in Africa', *International Affairs,* 78(3): 567-84

Mies, M. and Shiva, V. (1993) *Ecofeminism, Halifax, London; Atlantic Highlands,* Fernwood Publications; London, Zed Books

Monbiot, G. (2012) 'Dark hearts', *The Guardian,* 23 April, https://bit.ly/3DNZcqO, accessed 5 December 2022

Moyo, D. (2012) *L'aide fatale. Les ravages d'une aide inutile et de nouvelles solutions pour l'Afrique,* Paris, J.-C. Lattès

Ndlovu-Gatsheni, S.J. (2018) 'The dynamics of epistemological decolonisation in the 21st century: Towards epistemic freedom', *Strategic Review for Southern Africa,* 40(1): 16-45

Nunn, N. (2010) 'Religious conversion in colonial Africa', *American Economic Review,* vol. 100, no. 2:147-52

OECD (2021) 'Official Development Assistance (ODA)', n.d., https://www.oecd.org/dac/financing-sustainable-development/development-finance-standards/official-development-assistance.htm, accessed 5 December 2022

Pailey, R.N. (2020) 'De-centring the "White Gaze" of development', *Development and Change*, 51(3): 729-45

Parpart, J.L. (1995) 'Post-modernism, gender and development', In Crush, J. (ed), *Development and Power*, London, Routledge

Pierre, J. (2020) 'The racial vernaculars of development: A view from West Africa', *American Anthropologist,* 122(1): 86-98

Pieterse, J.N. (1992) *White on Black: Images of Africa and Blacks in Western Popular Culture*, New Haven, Yale University Press

Pieterse, J.N. and Parekh, B. (eds) (1995) *The Decolonization of Imagination: Culture, Knowledge and Power,* London, Atlantic Highlands, Zed Books

Sarr, F. (2016) *Afrotopia,* Paris, Philippe Rey

Shanin, T. (1997) 'The idea of progress', in Rahnema, M. (ed) *The Post-Development Reader*, London, Zed Books

Sondarjee, M. (2020) *Perdre Le Sud. Décoloniser La Solidarité Internationale*, Montreal, Éditions Écosociété

Spivak, G.C. (1988) 'Can the subaltern speak?', in Nelson, C. and Grossberg, L. (eds) *Marxism and the Interpretation of Culture,* pp. 271-313, Basingstoke, Macmillan

Stake, B. (2004) 'How far dare an evaluator go toward saving the world?', *American Journal of Evaluation*, 25(1): 103-7

Syed, J. and Ali, F. (2011) 'The White woman's burden: From colonial "civilisation" to third world "development"', *Third World Quarterly,* 32(2): 349-65

Tamale, S. (2020) *Decolonization and Afro-Feminism*, Ottawa, Daraja Press

White, S. (2002) 'Thinking race, thinking development', *Third World Quarterly*, 23(3): 407-19

Willer-Kherbaoui, J. (2019) *Working Through the Smog: How White Individuals Develop Critical Consciousness of White Saviorism*, North Andover, MA, Merrimack College

Wilson, K. (2012) Race, *Racism and Development: Interrogating History, Discourse and Practice*, London, New York, Zed Books; distributed in the USA exclusively by Palgrave Macmillan

Willuweit, F. (2020) 'De-constructing the "White Savior Syndrome": A manifestation of neo-imperialism', *E-International Relations*, 13 July, https://www.e-ir.info/pdf/86199, accessed 5 December 2022

PART I

THEORY AND PRACTICE

1

Indigenous Cultures and the Industrial-Colonial-Patriarchal White Savior Complex

Marcelo Saavedra-Vargas

*One song we hear too often is the one in which
Africa serves as a backdrop for White fantasies
of conquest and heroism ... a nobody from
America or Europe can go to Africa and become
a godlike savior or, at the very least,
have his or her emotional needs satisfied.*
Teju Cole (2012)

In a way, the modern world began abruptly for Indigenous people when alien humans set foot on our territories after crossing the Atlantic Ocean to what is now known as North America, departing from Palos in Spain in 1492. This was not a journey that would be filled with joy and happiness. On the contrary, this was the starting point of what we describe as the long nightmare of colonization: oppression, exploitation, genocide as never seen before and a constant minoritization of the Indigenous population, yet we are inextricably woven with our territories, lands, mountains, forests and body water.

Behind all these vile behaviors, we find the industrial-colonial-patriarchal White Savior Complex that has been pervading affluent societies since that terrible day when Christopher Columbus landed on the shores of the Americas. This invasion caught us unprepared, as we were following the original instructions of our elders. We never expected that there could be a sinister point of inflection that could imply so much suffering, exploitation, oppression and innumerable deaths, in addition to the deliberate dismantling of our whole realms of existence. Over five centuries have transpired, and our souls haven't stopped sobbing and remembering our Pachamama (hunting grounds) or our Wacas (ancestors).

Not even for a millisecond have we stopped resisting this alien invasion. We will never stop doing this, for we want to deliver to our children a viable world devoid of evil and all the vile systems of oppression the colonizers have tried so hard to imprint on our spirits. We stand in rebellion, following our grandmother Anacaona from the Taino nation, born in Xaragua, and the first of us that rose in arms against the evil forces that changed our realms of existence.

The issue of the greatest genocide ever, that of the Indigenous peoples of North America and beyond, goes beyond the scope of this chapter. But it is my moral duty to show and share my position on behalf of the millions of ancestors that were lost to the so-called 'Columbian Exchange'. The remains of hundreds of Indigenous children found across Canada in 2021 are only a token of the Mother of all Genocides. Ideological discussions take over when we speak of the atrocities committed by the European invaders.

This chapter chronicles the legacy of a Spanish conquistador, Bartolomé de las Casas, and one of those forces that changed our lives forever. He arrived in the early 16th century to be a settler but slowly started to denounce the atrocities done by his country to the Indigenous people in what is now known as the West Indies. His actions illustrate how the industrial-colonial-patriarchal White Savior Complex ingrained itself as far back as the conquest of North America over the Indigenous people of the continent. The chapter points at the irony of the genocides of Indigenous communities compared to the establishment of the League of Nations in 1920. In that period, there were hosts of young people ready to 'conquer' the world of the poor and spread the new gospel of liberal institutions. Thus, White Saviorism was developed following the model set out by de las Casas.

THE PSYCHOLOGICAL LEGACY OF
BARTOLOMÉ DE LAS CASAS

Bartolomé de las Casas, a Spanish conquistador who came to our territories in 1502 dressed up in friar's clothes, came to our lands with greed, avarice (MacNutt 2007) and a largely unsatisfied thirst for richness, prestige and political power. The literature consulted portrays the religious Bartolome de las Casas as 'the figure of a victor, who served God and loved his fellow-men' (*Ibid.*, p. 7) and helps us understand the ethos behind the modern industrial-colonial-patriarchal White Savior Complex, now unconsciously followed by scores of young saviors in the Western world who are not aware of the brutality that built its foundations.

In some cases, these young saviors even defied the colonial state by trying to push their good-intentioned agenda to help those who were forced to depend on the mercy of imperial forces. In the ongoing contest between the colonizer and the colonized (Fanon 1963), the supreme political, military, economic and social power was doubtlessly vested with the colonial metropolitan state. They 'ruled through a bureaucracy, of which the members were rarely efficient and usually corrupt. Hence it followed that Spaniards were bereft of any incentive to colonize, save one–their individual aggrandisement' (MacNutt 2007, p. 12).

Bartolomé de las Casas was the first White Savior who established the character of subsequent saviors coming from the First World to the Dispossessed Worlds. García (2011) argues that de las Casas constitutes the 'generation zero' in elaborating what the West considers the evolution of individual human rights (*Ibid.*, p. 1). Bartolomé de las Casas knew of Columbus' invasion when he was only nine years old, as he witnessed the return of the *Almirante de la Mar Océana* (Benet 2007, p. 13) to the shores of Sevilla, parading with 'great display of Indigenous people, parrots' The same year, his father Pedro returned with a Taíno slave, who stayed with the family for six years, until 1500. The Spanish colonies relied entirely on the Crown and were, from the outset, over-provided with royal cadres. These settlements generally owed their existence to private enterprise.

Friar Bartolomé de las Casas lived for a bit longer than eight decades. He lived a prolific life and experienced different journeys. Among other things, he was consecrated as a 'Servant of God' by the Roman Catholic Church in March 1554. The examples he set while alive configured a good priest and conditioned the major traits we attach to White Saviorism, who is someone mature enough, taking a course of life that, he assumes, will produce the best outcomes.

The industrial-colonial-patriarchal White Savior Complex was initiated by a contemplative mind who got terrorized by the atrocities committed by his fellow conquistadores in the pursuit of, mainly, wealth, recognition, status and the conversion of 'Indian' populations, coming from the recently 'discovered' New World. This contemplative mind belonged to friar Bartolomé de las Casas, who with his intervention foresaw the creation of multilateralism and the subsequent creation of the League of Nations, followed by the United Nations. However, he also planted the seed of what came to be known as the White Savior complex, which I qualify here, expanding its name to the industrial-patriarchal-colonial White Savior complex, and its symptomatology drives me to define it as a syndrome.

De las Casas attempted to reach a Utopia being entertained in his mind; something sort of an 'ideal colony': 'model Indians, adorned with primitive values' (MacNutt 2007, p. 10) (but highly validated by Christian ideology). Bartolomé's context is complicated, as usually Western social contexts are. He came from a European continent where civil and religious despotism was the proper way of dealing with things. The ruling despots were the ultimate instance of validation, and de las Casas was ahead of his times. His voice 'was incessantly raised in vindication of the inherent and inalienable right of every human being to the enjoyment of liberty'. He denounced the wrong-doings of people in positions of power since he was pre-eminently a person of action who claimed to understand the core of all humans, showing his 'universal' sympathy for people, gifted with an 'uncommon practical ability to devise corrective reforms that commanded the attention and won the approval of the foremost statesmen and moralists of his time' (*Ibid.*, p. 9).

De las Casas arrived in the continent as a settler, but upon realizing the atrocities being committed upon Indigenous peoples, he became wary of such practices. Because he was part of one of the ultimate colonial enterprises but then switched attitudes and wanted to 'save' Indigenous populations, he became a template for White Saviorism. With the power coming from Whiteness, he defended them, but while doing so, he advocated for a world where it was possible to develop more humane colonization practices. He wanted to 'help' them but never contested the core of the colonial structures.

Despite Bartolomé having been named protector of the Indians, he had in mind a specific social order for that protected place inhabited by Indians: this place was a utopia or 'ideal colony, peopled by perfect Christians labouring for the conversion of model Indians, adorned with primitive virtues' (*Ibid.*, p. 10). He assumed that Christianity was a universal religion, and that proper people were going to be Christians; it couldn't be otherwise. This is very contradictory to the multitude of religious beliefs in the ethnosphere.

THE INDIGENOUS GENOCIDE

The discovery of America was followed by possibly the greatest demographic disaster in the history of the world. (Denevan 1992)

The Abya-Yala is the main territory that encompassed all the territories populated by original tribes and cultures in the Kuna language (used by the Kuna nation). The meaning of this descriptor is 'the land in permanent fruition' or 'the mature territory'. This geography corresponds to those territories included from the Arctic, the Back of the Turtle, down through the Anahuak (the land between two bodies of water, in Nahuatl) and the Tawantinsuyu, down to the point of the Southern Cone. For us, the original Indigenous peoples of these lands, our territories have always been there, are supporting the deployment of our personal and collective beings over the land. For instance, the Algonquin nation has been growing roots on their territories for the past 8,500 years. The Aymara nation has been weaving their stories on the land for more than 5,000 years. We had names that reflected our mature mutual acknowledgment with the territories.

A massive genocide took place in Abya-Yala, despite the efforts deployed by Bartolome de las Casas. Europe and Euroamerican saviors and organizations devised to mitigate the murderous effects of the imposition of a host of systems of oppression, which included the deliberate annihilation of our ancestors via diverse methods of 'killing the Indian while saving the man'.[1] This genocide was made with the support of the Church. In 1452, Pope Nicholas V issued a papal bull *Dum Diversas*[2]–a decree declaring war on all non-Christians around the world and approving and encouraging the conquest, colonization and exploitation of non-Christian nations and their territories. Pope Nicholas' bull also decreed that Christians had the right to 'capture, conquer and subdue the Saracens, pagans and other enemies of Christ, to put them in perpetual slavery' and 'to take all their possessions and property...'[3]

Scholarly estimates of the size of the post-Columbian holocaust have climbed sharply in recent decades (Stannard 1992, p. 10), to get closer to the numbers proposed by a number of Indigenous scholars, including me, who argue that in the Abya-Yala we were close to 100-150 million peoples. I

---

[1] Richard H. Pratt spoke about this policy of extermination in a speech delivered in 1892 in the 'History Matters' Conference at George Mason University, Fairfax, VA, USA.

[2] *Dum Diversas* (until different in English) is a papal bull from 1452 by Pope Nicholas V. It authorized Afonso V of Portugal to conquer Saracens and pagans and consign them to 'perpetual servitude'. Pope Calixtus III reiterated it in 1456 with Inter Caetera (not to be confused with Alexander VI's), renewed by Pope Sixtus IV in 1481 and Pope Leo X in 1514 with Precelse denotionis. The concept of the consignment of exclusive spheres of influence to certain nation-states was extended to the Americas in 1493 by Pope Alexander VI with *Inter caetera*.

[3] *Romanis Pontifex* by Pope Nicholas V to King Afonso V of Portugal, 1455.

understand that we were 120 million original peoples, considering the so-called 'isolated' tribes of Amazonia, living and coexisting in equilibrium and harmony with what surrounded us. After having conducted research with other Indigenous elders, I carried out my own statistical research based on what my elders shared with me. In the Akimínak Nimítik (Algonquian language), there were approximately 18 million inhabitants distributed among more than 500 nations. The Europeans, instead of admiring and developing justice-based relations with the original peoples, tried to bring them to annihilation, greatly accomplishing this task and reducing more than 500 Indigenous nations to racial minorities. After a hundred years transpired, in 1595, there were about 1 million people left. Now, over 400 years later, and nowadays, there are only 1,673,785 Indigenous peoples remaining in Canada (Statistics Canada 2016). The rate of extinction is thus 94.4 and 90.7 percent, respectively.

The Grand Genocide that took place in the Abya-Yala has no paragon on this planet; once in matter of few years, many human nations were pushed to extinction by greed enshrined in the European heart and responding to the images, they held in their minds about the nature of the persons found in what they called the New World. Despite de las Casas' best efforts, or perhaps because of them, one of the world's biggest tragedies took place. His White Savior's actions did not trigger the end of this genocide, but instead gave precedence to a type of attitude that perpetuates this White Saviorism without criticizing a system based on the exploitation of Indigenous peoples.

WHITE SAVIORISM AFTER WORLD WAR I

A collapsing Western paradigm is occurring in parallel as the industrial modern civilization is being brought down, mimicking how colonialism came to exist, tightly holding the epistemological hand of its twin brother, capitalism. Together they managed to push life on this vessel planet to the brink of a catastrophic collapse. Social scientists call this the Anthropocene (the geological era of humans), blaming us all without considering, for instance, that the ecological footprint of a Canadian newborn is a hundred times that of a Bengali newborn.

The term White Savior, which is sometimes combined with complex to write White Savior Complex, refers to a White person, assumed to come from the developed world, North America or Europe, who provides help to non-White people, often in the Global South, in a self-serving manner. The role is considered a modern-day version of what is expressed in the poem 'The White Man's Burden' by Rudyard Kipling (1899). Writer Teju Cole combined the term with 'industrial complex' (derived from the military-industrial complex and similarly applied elsewhere) to coin 'White Savior Industrial Complex'. I use this qualifying descriptor, adding to it that beyond being only a complex, it is a set of traits, complexes and symptomatology, including the patriarchal oppression system that sits as the platform for many other oppressive scaffoldings: the industrial-colonial-patriarchal White Savior Complex.

The White Saviorism discourse usually comes from the minds of those that come from the Western developed world, subjugated by Judeo-Christian beliefs similar to that of de las Casas. They enjoy the privileges that the modern world offers, as a result of more than five centuries of relentless exploitation, extraction and oppression and the theft of, what they term 'natural resources'[4] (Frey 2016). In modern nomenclature, the 'First World' was assigned to the developed capitalist nation-states; the 'Second World' was supposed to be nation-states trying to attain socialism; the 'Third World' were nation-states that didn't comply with either of the previously mentioned worlds. However, there were important pockets of the population made up of Indigenous peoples living in the so-called First World, where the standards of living were quite high, yet they lived in sub-human, Third World-like conditions. This is a testimony of the failed market capitalist systems and the fictional nature of what it promises.

Because of its very nature, a vertical relationship ensues when a privileged colonizer from the First World meets a Third or Fourth World dispossessed person or community. It has been like since the Columbian Exchange made three utterly dissimilar worlds (Africa, Abya-Yala and Europe) that relate to each other by following an unwritten colonial pact.[5]

Dealing with White Saviorism implies we start reformulating the colonized mentalities we have been brewed in and following the seminal works of Albert Memmi[6] and Frantz Fanon, whom I recognize as having unveiled the various layers of psychological predispositions as colonizers and colonized.

---

[4] We don't use the term resources in the ethnosphere. Rather, they are blessings, gifts and relations showing the sanctity of our ultimate provider, mother nature, or Pachamama.

[5] In rigor, the so-called 'colonial pact' was an understanding between imperial and colonist France and its subservient colonies, by which the latter would have to put 85 per cent of their foreign reserve into France Central Bank', under the control of the French minister of finance. (Eight West African countries rename currency in historic break from France, *Global Voices*, 2021.)

[6] The colonizer and the colonized.

We also need to venture into the realm of history, historiography and cartography of that age and find out how the European mentality was predisposed to at the end of the 15th century and how they viewed humans from other latitudes. That was the age of 'exploration and discovery', that we, from a perspective of mature cultures, should call it the age of imperial expansion, amazement and invasion or *veni, vide, vici*.[7] The publications of that time are very telling about the imaginary dressing up of the European mind, before they 'discovered' the so-called New World.

Also known as the Woodcut of Nuremberg, the Nuremberg Chronicle was published in the year after Columbus set foot on the Abya-Yala. It gives us a peek at the European psyche at the end of the 15th century. A look at the world that persists up to modern days; although some features and misconceptions were 'corrected' over time, the minds that produced it can still be found in the psychological profiles of Euro-Americans as well as the minds of colonized populations. The description of this first encyclopedia reads:

> The Nuremberg Chronicle is an illustrated encyclopaedia consisting of world historical accounts, as well as accounts told through biblical paraphrase. Subjects include human history in relation to the bible, illustrated mythological creatures, and the histories of important Christian and secular cities from antiquity. Finished in 1493 after years in the making, it is one of the best-documented early printed books—an incunabulum—and one of the first to successfully integrate illustrations and text.

Overall, Indigenous nations have a totally different perception of this invasion perpetrated by European colonial forces. This

---

[7] Plutarch, Life of Caesar from penelope.uchicago.edu: The phrase is attributed in Plutarch's Life of Caesar and Suetonius's Lives of the Twelve Caesars: Julius. Plutarch writes that Caesar used it in a report to Amantius, a friend of his in Rome.

is clearly the vision of conquerors and victors. Although we are considered victims, and we have been, these are the times of awakening to our cosmic belonging. It's a simple and basic truth that acquired real existence for 529 years. The industrial-colonial-patriarchal White Savior Complex has been around throughout history, trying to depict invading colonizers as benefactors that brought civility to barbarians.

It was also reinforced in the interwar period between the two world wars. Based on the Treaty of Versailles (10 January 1920), the League of Nations met for the first time on 16 January 1920 and was dissolved on 20 April 1946 to give place to the United Nations. Once the League of Nations came into existence, the consequent United Nations system found its bases to become a global government-like set of administrators who were, among other things, set to help marginalized populations. For Indigenous peoples, it represents the ongoing process of colonialism, acquiring new forms. The new actor was an authority in defining development: the USA way of life. Western young people were ready to save / conquer the poor and spread liberalism. The White Savior mentality set out by Bartolomé de las Casas was thus reinforced.

CONCLUSION

We have peeked at the mind frames of the European invader. We can easily sense they were permeated with a set of beliefs that portrayed a world filled with anomalies, proto-humanoids, monstrosities and a religious belief system based on a single set of perspectives that made them incapable of relating to other forms of life around the planet.

Blinded by their ideologies and epistemologies, the invaders were unable to appreciate the wonderful world they were 'discovering', the real equilibrium we sustained with what surrounds our existences and the harmony with which we approach a reality that was close to our 'hunting grounds'. Instead, they orchestrated one of the worst genocides in history while some tried to 'help' Indigenous populations and civilize them. Doing so, they wiped out much of Indigenous existence and harmony with nature.

We all call this planet our ultimate mother, Pachamama: we come from her and embedded in our spirits, we can easily find the four sacred elements. As much as the Western mind fights against this mutual belonging with nature, they keep on failing and provoking calamitous changes in the geological scale. We are risking to devoid this home planet of life as a massive extinction event is already underway. It's a dreadful reality. We are going through this planet's sixth period of plant and animal mass extinction, including those that inhabit the oceans; the sixth to happen in the last 500 million years. The current wave is considered to be the worst series of species elimination since the dinosaurs disappeared 65 million years ago to a celestial body, Xilubut, in the Mayan language.

Extinction is a phenomenon that occurs naturally; however, it normally happens at a rate of 1-5 species every year. But, as scientists estimate (WAF 2022), we are currently losing species 1,000-10,000 times faster than that, which means that literally tens of species are vanishing from the face of the Earth every day. We could be looking at a frightening present. By this rate, almost one-third to one-half of all species could become extinct by 2050.

The desperate actions propelled by young Westerners living in the so-called First World have no effect on the huge disparities they dream to change, mainly due to the scale of our current geological age and the ineffectiveness of their intentions, which probably augment the disaster. The destruction provoked by insatiable greed paired with powerful technologies and increasing extractive innovation leaves behind an enormous ecological footprint in which our desperate actions do not make a dent. Even more, the small changes that White Saviorism manages to bring about are largely upset by the net effect of their action, which tends to increase the huge divide between rich nation-states and the poor. What is actually spent in this remediation carried out with good intent by those young people finances the administration of 'humanitarian' agencies and development organizations, perpetuating the 'colonial pact'.

What to do? Decolonize minds so young people can actually become good allies, and we take on the dismantling of the colonial realities together. These teachings are largely in the hands of mature Indigenous cultures, and we will share what we are with anyone who is willing to coexist together. They need to acknowledge that there are cultures that have already matured and are wise enough to guide our actions and allow us to avoid the Anthropocene by understanding that we have prevailed in time to keep the wisdom of our species alive and feel empowered to create a new social order. Our young, if well mentored and guided, need to be good ancestors.

REFERENCES

Benet, P.I.F. (2007) 'Cristóbal Colón: vida y viajes del Gran Almirante de las Indias: síntesis histórica / escrita con presencia de las obras de los más eminentes autores por M. Pons Fábregues', Alicante, *Biblioteca Virtual Miguel de Cervantes*; Madrid, Biblioteca Nacional

Cole, T. (2012) 'The White Savior industrial complex', *The Atlantic,* 21 March

Denevan, W.M. (1992) *The Native Populations of the Americas in 1492*, Madison, University of Wisconsin Press

Fanon, F. (1963) *The Wretched of the Earth*, New York, Grove Press

Frey, C.J. (2016) 'The White Savior in the mirror', *Annual Review of Comparative and International Education*, vol. 30:185-98

García García, E. (2011) 'Bartolomé de Las Casas y los Derechos Humanos', in *Los Derechos Humanos en su origen*, Aletheia, (52):81-114

Kipling, R. (1899) 'The White man's burden', *McClure's Magazine*, n.d.

MacNutt, F.A. (2007) *Bartholomew de Las Casas; His Life, Apostolate, and Writings*, Cleveland, USA, The Arthur H. Clark Company

Stannard, D. (1992) *American Holocaust: The Conquest of the New World*, Oxford, Oxford University Press

Statistics Canada (2016) '2016 census topic: Aboriginal peoples', https://www12.statcan.gc.ca/census-recensement/2016/rt-td/ap-pa-eng.cfm, accessed 24 March 2022

World Animal Foundation (WAF) (2022) 'Extinction crisis', https://worldanimalfoundation.org/wild-earth/extinction-crisis/#:~:text=The%20world%20is%20facing%20an,future%20of%20life%20on%20earth, accessed 5 December 2022

2

Evaluation and the White Gaze in International Development

Sadaf Shallwani and Shama Dossa

E valuation has long been considered an essential part of international development, as it seeks to assess the effectiveness, efficiency and impact of different interventions. Global development is increasingly being critiqued for perpetuating neo-colonial, imperial, neoliberal and racist agendas, and we believe that the principles and practices of evaluation are important tools in service of these agendas. In this chapter, we argue that many of the principles and practices of evaluation are tools for the White gaze, which is rooted in White supremacy and serves the narrative of White Saviorism. Evaluation in global development centers on the White subject as the doer, the Savior and the neutral expert. It establishes Whiteness as the norm, identifies deficits and problems in the lives of Black and Brown people and demonstrates how interventions designed and funded by the Global North are necessary and effective–thereby reinforcing the 'feel good' element of the White Saviorism. Furthermore, the White gaze contorts the purposes and ethics of evaluation. While couched in the discourse of 'accountability' and 'evidence-based' decision-making, evaluation implicitly serves as a tool for White surveillance and intervention on Brown and Black lives in the Global South.

Evaluators of color from both the Global South and Global North are also trained to internalize these views, assumptions and practices and participate as agents and 'foot soldiers' for the neo-colonial project of international development. In fact, in this chapter, wherever we refer to White people, we also include people of color, especially in positions of power, who take on elements of Whiteness in their actions. People of color have been rewarded by White supremacy for aligning themselves with White norms, worldviews and approaches and have, therefore, often been complicit in reinforcing White supremacy and reproducing White Saviorism.

As the authors, we are aware of the fact that we are hybrid (Global South / North) women researchers of color and we recognize our own role in using–and in trying to subvert–the tools of evaluation. We also appreciate the limits of using the 'master's tools' (Lorde 1983) and the importance of building and strengthening alternative discourses, approaches and methodologies. Decolonizing evaluation requires engaging with imperialism and colonialism at multiple levels and in multiple ways. It also requires a critical reflexive analysis of the assumptions, motivations and values that underpin evaluation practices. This chapter is part of our own critical reflexive practice as evaluators in global development.

THE WHITE GAZE IN INTERNATIONAL DEVELOPMENT

The White gaze is the notion that subjects draw on a particular (White) lens to observe, analyze and intervene in the lives of Brown and Black objects–whose agency is, as a result, minimized. We argue that the White gaze is not just about passive observation but rather it is active, and intentional and has a lasting impact on the object of the gaze.

Pailey (2020) explains that in global development,

> [The White gaze] assumes whiteness as the primary referent of power, prestige and progress. It equates whiteness with wholeness and superiority. The 'white gaze' of development measures the political, socio-economic and cultural processes of Southern black, brown and other people of colour against a standard of Northern whiteness and finds them incomplete, wanting, inferior or regressive. (p. 5)

A critical analysis shows the White gaze is manifest across many, if not all, aspects of global development (see Box 1 for some examples).

White supremacy is the unnamed political system that underlies the White gaze in development and White Saviorism with which the White gaze is intertwined. The narrative presumes that the White 'developed' and 'civilized' world is what the Global South should aspire to. As will be discussed in this chapter, White supremacy equates Whiteness with legitimacy, innocence, benevolence, objectivity and knowledge and expertise. In doing so, it justifies White people and White-led organizations having greater access to opportunities, privilege, credibility and higher levels of pay and security.

EVALUATION AS THE WHITE GAZE IN DEVELOPMENT

Evaluation has been defined as a set of systematic processes to use evidence to judge the merit, worth or significance of an initiative. Specifically, evaluation aims to assess a project or initiative's achievement of its objectives, as well as its efficiency, effectiveness, impact and sustainability.

Evaluation as a discipline has roots in Western empirical traditions. Most texts and models that describe how best to evaluate programmes come from the Global North. They set out rules and frameworks that specify what proper evaluation is, how evaluation should be done and what constitutes valid knowledge. According to Alkin (2013), the origins of the field of evaluation are rooted in a rationale for improved programmes for the benefit of society, establishing systematic and scientific methods and presenting the 'truth'.[1]

Historically, evaluation models have been based on methods found in the physical sciences, such as randomized control trials (RCTs), which are presented to date as the 'gold standard' (*Ibid.*). As Western scientific thought began expanding to consider post-positivism, constructivist evaluation theory opened up to the possibilities of challenging notions of truth and reality. Qualitative approaches gradually began to be included alongside quantitative methods, followed by participatory, empowerment and user-centered approaches. However, this has also been accompanied by global political agendas and growing neoliberal concerns around governance and efficiency. These are manifested in funders' requirements for stringent monitoring as well as evaluation methods that analyze and maximize measurable results (Global Affairs Canada 2016) and 'value for money' (UK AID Direct 2019). Interestingly, cost-benefit analysis in evaluation actually originates from military defense contractors like the Rand Corporation, who first used the model to allocate United States Department of Defence budgets to weapons systems that would optimize military objectives (Levin 2013).

---

[1] Alkin's narrative of evaluation's origins has been critiqued for further institutionalizing and perpetuating the Whiteness of evaluation theory and practice. Importantly, the contributions of people of colour, Indigenous people, and/or people from the Global South are largely missing from this narrative.

Box 1: How does the White gaze manifest in development? Some examples.

→ White people talking to other White people about Black and Brown people's lives and contexts, telling their stories and / or making decisions that affect Black and Brown peoples' lives.

→ Approaches and tools rooted in White, Western values, worldviews and knowledge systems, being applied to the lives of Brown and Black people in the Global South, while disregarding or minimizing local and Indigenous knowledge.

→ White 'experts' providing direction to and / or approving / giving credibility to the perspectives and actions of Brown and Black people.

→ Organizations led by White people being funded to 'build the capacity' of 'local' (Black or Brown-led) organizations.

→ White people's entitlement and confidence in travelling to diverse contexts across the Global South to 'help'—without thinking about the ways in which they are centring themselves, and the disruption and harm caused to the communities and countries with whom they are interacting.

→ The instrumentalization of Black and Brown people's pain, trauma, narratives and stories of success for the White gaze, in order to appeal to the emotions and wallets of White people.

Evaluation, along with research and monitoring, is an important tool that perpetuates the White gaze in global development. According to Smith (2012), research through 'imperial eyes' (what we call the White gaze) centers on a Western worldview, conveys superiority and entitlement and is driven by a desire to bring 'progress' into the lives of Indigenous peoples—who are viewed as lacking. This approach 'steals' knowledge from Indigenous peoples, and its primary benefits are accrued by those who 'stole' it.

In the following sections, we describe how we have observed the White gaze manifest in evaluation systems and processes in international development: in centering the White subject, in the production and use of 'knowledge' and in the purpose and ethics of evaluation.

THE WHITE GAZE CENTERS THE WHITE SUBJECT

The White gaze centers White people as the subjects (the doers, the agents) of interventions and studies, and Black and Brown people and other people of color as the objects–upon whose lives interventions and studies occur. For example, development research studies on Global South contexts are usually led by researchers from the Global North, and many (see Rees *et al.*, 2021)–in some cases, the majority (see Liverpool 2021)–do not include any Global South researchers. Similarly, funders and International Non-Governmental Organizations (INGOs) often appoint White evaluators to lead evaluations of their interventions.

Evaluation reports are also generally written for consumption by White audiences–such as Global North funders and INGOs. We have both had experiences conducting in-depth and participatory evaluations that resulted in rich data and insightful collaborative analysis with communities. However, the primary feedback from the funders who commissioned them was to substantially shorten the reports as the funder did not have time to read them. The time of the donor and the idea of efficiency were considered more important than the depth and nuance of what communities felt was important to share.

The centering of Whiteness also gives greater value to the lives and safety of White 'expats' over Black or Brown nationals. For example, as an evaluator of color, I (Shama) have found that I am regularly paid less and expected to take on a higher level of risk in the field, compared to my White 'expat' colleagues–often less qualified–who receive more pay and security protection. These experiences illustrate how the White subject is considered more valuable and worthy of protection, while Black and Brown lives are treated as more expendable.

Three fundamental assumptions regarding the White subject are integral to the White gaze–that they are helping and doing good (White Saviorism), that they are neutral and unbiased and that they are globally relevant 'experts'. We describe these each in turn below.

First, White Saviorism centers on the benevolence of the White subject who has come to help poor and needy people in the Global South. Evaluation and research contribute to White Saviorism by establishing 'deficit' and 'need' in communities of color and Indigenous communities to justify intervention. Evaluators document change and impact through numbers and stories and provide gratification to the White funders and INGOs who have provided support–all while deftly avoiding addressing issues of structural inequity and harmful systems, which may make the White Saviors uncomfortable or accountable. And fundamentally, evaluators working in international development, just as White Savior practitioners, view themselves as 'good people', who 'contribute to the making of a better world' (Stake 2004, p. 103).

Second, the White subject is considered to be neutral and unbiased–an important requisite for evaluation and research, which require 'objectivity' and 'independence' (United Nations Evaluation Group 2020). This premise of objectivity assumes, first, that it is possible as a human being to genuinely step out of one's own contextually developed and biased understanding of the world to do research or evaluation (it's not); second, that White people from the Global North are neutral actors in international development (they're not) and, third, that independence and neutrality are always desirable (they're not).

Third, in international development, White people tend to be treated as experts–as more knowledgeable and skilled, and with knowledge and skills that are globally relevant in multiple contexts outside their own. In addition to the expertise inherently assumed in Whiteness, knowledge, training and experience obtained in Global North settings are often considered to be universally valid and applicable. At the same time, that same global relevance is not afforded to similar knowledge and experiences obtained from Global South institutions.

We have countless examples of White people exhibiting confidence in the relevance and applicability of their expertise to contexts outside their own–because the sector treats them as global experts. For example, I (Sadaf) have mostly had White, Global North supervisors in my academic and professional roles, despite their global scope. This has meant that I have had to constantly convince my White supervisors of the methods I use and the validity of my findings and interpretations–as they assess my work according to White, Western norms of research / evaluation and practice. It has also meant that I was not challenged and held accountable for how I myself might be unintentionally perpetuating White norms and supremacy in my methods, findings and interpretations. Many of these White leaders–while skilled and experienced in their own right–have not, to my knowledge, questioned their suitability to supervise researchers or practitioners of color working in the Global South and essentially direct international activity in a multitude of contexts outside and different from their own.

We are aware of endless examples of well-compensated White consultants being flown in from North America or

Europe, using a few limited interactions to evaluate a program in a Global South context. These consultants make recommendations that have real implications for strategy, resourcing and methods–and on the lives of Brown and Black people in the Global South. In contrast, researchers and evaluators from the Global South are often treated as experts only in their own country's context, if that. When they are enabled access to global roles, this access largely tends to be reserved for those with education and passports from the Global North (the 'White' privilege of people of color having certain nationalities) (Kallman 2019), and these roles still generally focus on other Global South contexts. It is virtually unheard of for a Global South consultant to be brought in to assess, analyze and provide judgment on social issues and programs in communities in the Global North.

Our own education and connections to the Global North have afforded us some privileges of Whiteness as well. As a Canadian graduate student doing an internship with an INGO's regional office in Kenya, I (Sadaf) was asked to observe, evaluate and document some of their local programs. Based on my observations, I was also invited to conduct training for the practitioners–many with decades more experience than myself. My proximity to Whiteness through my education from the Global North conferred me expertise despite having hardly any prior experience in East African contexts. Reflecting on this, I feel embarrassed for having participated in and benefited from this enactment of the White subject. I am grateful for the increased humility, nuanced understanding and critical reflexive practice I have developed since then, largely due to Brown and Black colleagues in the Global South who teach me and hold me accountable.

THE WHITE GAZE SHAPES THE
PRODUCTION AND USE OF KNOWLEDGE

We now turn to how the White gaze influences the production and use of knowledge. The White gaze shapes how issues are conceptualized, understood and measured by establishing Whiteness as the norm and the White Western world as the centre of legitimate knowledge. The White gaze focuses on perceived deficits in Brown and Black people and defines success and how it can be measured. The White gaze further determines what is considered valid knowledge and valid evidence through the technocratization of the field of evaluation and its methods. We describe each of these in turn below.

First, the White gaze relies on imagining White bodies, lives, experiences, perspectives and 'progress' as the universal norm. For example, conceptualizations of human rights, optimal family structures, values and human development trajectories are often developed in Global North contexts and then exported as universal across the globe. The terminology around 'development' also implies that development is linear and that the 'developed' state of many Global North countries and cultures is what 'developing' countries in the Global South should aspire for and work towards. Although this linearity in development has been critiqued, it is still heavily reflected in the ways in which development projects are designed and evaluated, with their theories of change and logic models.

In addition, as Smith (2012) notes, the White / Western world centers and affirms itself as the center of legitimate, 'universal' knowledge. This is true for research findings and knowledge that the global development industry builds interventions upon. For example, in my (Sadaf's) experience, Global North research on child development and early interventions has been used as the foundation for early childhood development best practices and programs across the globe, usually with only superficial adaptation to the local context. As well, assessment tools from Western contexts–or developed for global contexts but by White researchers from the Global North–are widely used to assess children's development or the quality of early childhood programs. Predictably, these approaches and tools usually show children, parents and communities in the Global South doing 'poorly' compared to those in the Global North.

It is important to note that Global South scholars have actively resisted this knowledge imperialism for many decades. In recent years, there has been increasing recognition of the validity and value of Indigenous knowledge and practices, along with the need to disrupt what is considered to be universal but is actually primarily White / Western 'knowledge' and 'best practices' (Kjørholt and Penn 2019).

Second, the White gaze tends to focus–in both intervention and evaluation–on what are considered to be problematic social norms, values and cultural practices among Brown and Black people–thereby placing the deficit in the personhood and culture of the 'Other' rather than recognizing the broader local and global historic and current socioeconomic systems, contexts and dynamics that shape current situations. For example, in our experience of the early childhood space in global development, there is more emphasis on training people in responsive caregiving and positive parenting practices (i.e., improving people who are considered to have deficits in parenting or educating their young children), rather than addressing structural factors–both local and global–that keep families and children in poverty, food insecurity and marginalization. Similarly, in the child protection space, White funders and INGOs are passionate about changing cultural norms to end child marriage. While this is important, there is usually no acknowledgment of colonization (including the influence of Christianity in propagating patriarchal norms) or the racist and capitalist theft of people and wealth that have spread poverty and weakened government infrastructure across much of the Global South. Moreover, there is also little acknowledgment of local leaders, scholars, human rights activists, feminist movements, policymakers and practitioners who have been engaging in critical, contextually grounded change efforts for decades. Fundamentally, the White gaze collects, interprets and presents data and stories around the supposed deficits and needs of Brown and Black people in the Global South to satisfy the White Saviorism narrative.

Third, the White gaze defines success–how it is conceptualized, understood and measured. It usually defines progress as change that brings Black and Brown people's bodies and lives closer to what White people deem is the norm, desired and ideal. It further reproduces the neoliberal discourse with an emphasis on cost-effectiveness and scalability. It seeks to reduce complex social change processes to simple input–output–outcome interventions that show rapid results (e.g., as in 'results-based management' or the logical framework) and can and should be replicated and scaled across diverse contexts.

The White gaze's imagining of Whiteness as the norm, its focus on deficits in Brown and Black people's lives, and its emphasis on linear, measurable change, ignores the wealth and plurality of capacities and assets that Brown and Black people and communities have, silences or limits people's agency to discuss and describe their own realities on their own terms, and boxes people's lives into specific quantified indicators or case studies which serve to show change attributed to the development intervention.

In addition, the White gaze controls what is considered valid knowledge and valid evidence through the technocratization of the field of evaluation and its methods. Evaluation practices reproduce colonial approaches of counting and categorizing, making judgments and using those judgments to justify interventions in the lives of Indigenous people (Rivas 2018). This technocratization has resulted in the privileging of a specific kind of expertise developed in the Global North, over a plurality of other methods of knowledge generation.

Some of the specific skills and technical methodologies considered essential for robust evaluation practice include quantitative data collection and analysis skills; proficiency with specific language and tools, such as theories of change, logic models and log frames; statistical approaches to establish sample sizes; 'specific, measurable, achievable, relevant and time-bound' (SMART) indicators; cost–benefit or value-for-money analyses; writing case studies; and the ability to articulate specific and clear recommendations from findings. These technocratic practices foster elitism and rigidity rather than humility and flexibility among evaluators who internalize them, amplifying technocratically skilled evaluators' influence on programs and people's lives and disregarding Indigenous and Global South ways of generating knowledge and capturing evidence.

This technocratization also narrows the pedagogy and training that shape emerging evaluators, even in the Global South. Evaluation courses focus on prescribed methods and tools and often do not foster ethical, critical, abstract or creative thinking. Mainstream evaluation pedagogy generally does not encourage critical interrogation of these methods of knowledge production, nor does it value Indigenous methods of knowledge generation and transmission or encourage reflexive practice around the values and goals of the evaluation.

Evaluations are also considered more rigorous when carried out by an evaluator external to the project because they are perceived to be independent and, thus, objective. Credibility and validity further grow when the external evaluator is White or from the Global North (as discussed earlier around the assumption of the White subject as neutral). While even the supposed objectivity of an external party needs to be questioned, the underlying assumption here is that subjectivity and reflexivity are always negative. The reality is that social change is deeply complex and subjective, and there are many nuances and processes that 'insiders' can have a profoundly insightful understanding and analysis around that an external evaluator would not be able to fully grasp.

Evaluators of color from the Global South who identify, speak and act according to the prescribed norms also benefit from some of the privileges accorded to the technocratic elite in the field of evaluation. We (the authors) have both been educated as researchers to the Ph.D. level at Global North universities, and we are reflecting on how we have participated in and benefited from this technocracy–for example, by enabling our access to secure and esteemed roles leading evaluation and research for local and international development organizations. We also recognize that our multiple privileges enable us to speak about, disrupt and push back against White supremacy and neo-colonialism in the evaluation sector, such as in writing this chapter. This kind of reflexive practice, however, is usually discouraged in mainstream research and evaluation to maintain the facade of objectivity.

THE WHITE GAZE CONTORTS THE PURPOSES
AND ETHICS OF EVALUATION

The purported purpose of evaluation is to assess the effectiveness of a development intervention, usually to inform decisions about continuing, adapting and / or replicating it. However, there are other implicit purposes and values that underpin evaluation in global development, many of which serve and reinforce the underlying power structure of White supremacy (see Box 2 on the next page).

These reflections raise questions about the ethical considerations that might guide evaluators. While there are a couple of documents with ethical guidelines specifically for evaluators (United Nations Evaluation Group 2020), a study by Williams (2016), commissioned by UKAID (now the Foreign and Commonwealth Development Office or FCDO) and focused on UKAID-affiliated evaluators in global development, found that evaluators generally lacked a shared understanding of what ethics in evaluation are, the role of ethics in evaluation; and where the responsibility for ensuring ethical practice lies. These findings are consistent with our own experiences in the sector at large.

This lack of a coherent understanding of ethics among evaluators in global development results, at best, in a biased implementation of ethics and, at worst, allows for unchecked abuses of power, including the misuse of data. We further argue that ethical considerations need to dive deeper into questions of power, structural racism, knowledge production and ownership and the fundamental purposes and assumptions underlying evaluation.

Box 2.

Implicit purposes of evaluation in global development that reinforce White supremacy

→ One-way accountability from the recipient of funding to the (White) funder. The one with more power (usually the White-led Global North funder or INGO) is virtually never accountable to the one with less power.

→ Providing fuel for the (White) donor, leader or practitioner to 'feel good' about the change they made happen.

→ Placing the perceived 'deficit' in the 'Other's' culture and norms, while 'White washing' historic and current power structures built on race such as colonization, slavery and imperialism.

→ Surveillance—whereby the White subject and its organization and / or nation state monitor and document the lives of Brown and Black people, with the power to judge and intervene where they deem necessary. (*I (Shama) have experienced situations where a funder required excessive personal data from people with whom we worked, without clarity around where this data would go, who would have access to it and how it would be used. The skewed power relationships did not enable any questioning of these requirements nor any discussion on the ethics and security risks of such data collection.*)

→ Enabling (White) technocratic evaluators to build knowledge and data repositories, reputation, publications and wealth through roles in the global development sector—based on data extracted from people and communities in the Global South who often do not see much meaningful change in their day-to-day lives. (*Nithya Ramanathan calls this 'data colonialism'—'when one entity () claims ownership of data that is produced by others or for others, and also takes most of the value of that data' in this webinar hosted by Skoll.org, Decolonizing Data, 2021, https://www.youtube.com/watch? v=ue1MEW5Exhc*)

MOVING FORWARD

We propose five major strategies to dismantle the White gaze and help 'decolonize' evaluation. First, dismantling the White gaze requires explicitly talking about racism (Pailey 2020), including White supremacy, to identify where and how it shows up, how it harms and perpetuates harmful systems and how we can disrupt it. Recent efforts in evaluation include the #EvalSoWhite hashtag on Twitter, drawing attention to the dominance of White evaluators and approaches in development. Similarly, a call to action was made by hundreds of evaluators across the globe to the editors and publishers of a forthcoming edition of an edited book, *Evaluation Roots: A Wider Perspective of Theorists' Views and Influence*, originally published in 2012, on the 'roots' of evaluation to be more inclusive of Indigenous evaluation theory and practice, and to explicitly discuss colonialism and structural racism.

Second, a more authentic understanding of any community, situation or intervention requires consideration and analysis of the larger context. This includes historic and current systems of power–both local and global–that perpetuate racial inequity and harm people of color in the Global South. This means, for example, understanding and integrating how colonization, slavery, structural racism and imperialism–as well as capitalism, neoliberalism, patriarchy, religious dominance and other structures of power–have shaped current realities in specific local contexts, as well as in global patterns and dynamics.

Third, as a sector, we need to deeply engage with and reimagine the purposes and ethics of evaluation and embrace humility, pluralism and collaboration as guiding values. This requires recognizing the multiple ways of knowing, the implicit underpinnings in our approaches, the power and

58

responsibility that comes with generating and using knowledge for social change and to disrupt harmful systems, and the critical importance of entrusting the power of knowledge generation to people and communities most impacted by it. Redefining the purposes and ethics of evaluation will also enable us to set up more appropriate systems and processes for questioning, reflection and accountability regarding ethically sound approaches to evaluation.

Fourth, by interrogating and unpacking many current taken-for-granted assumptions, best practices and criteria for 'proper' evaluations, we can create space for a more meaningful understanding of good evaluation practice. For example, we might redefine good evaluation practice as that which is respectful and non-extractive, recognizes power dynamics, appreciates and meaningfully enables the participation and ownership of people and communities most impacted, and draws upon multiple ways of knowing and multiple forms of knowledge. This re-imagining also allows us to appreciate and learn from lived experiences (in addition to technical training) of evaluators and to expand the skills and capacities we foster and nurture in new evaluators. This allows us as evaluators to move beyond specific technocratic skills to include aspects such as understanding social justice, critical thinking relating to the specifics of the project as well as the larger local and global context, respectful and flexible approaches to learning from and integrating Indigenous ways of knowing and commitment to and skills in facilitating community ownership and engagement.

We also need to facilitate engagement among evaluators, practitioners and funders with the plurality of approaches to evaluation and knowledge generation–particularly those that support a transformative, social justice and solidarity agenda, such as participatory, Indigenous and feminist approaches. We caution, however, against co-opting the language and superficial implementation of any of these alternative approaches (for example–the way 'participatory evaluation' has been co-opted by Global North-dominated international organizations) without genuine commitment and action to make meaningful changes to power structures or taking political stances that would genuinely improve citizen ownership, agency and participation in society.

Finally, as we dismantle the White gaze, de-center the White subject and disrupt White Saviorism, we simultaneously need to take intentional, strong and consistent action to centre the worldviews, expertise, agency, lived experiences and perspectives of Black and Brown communities in the Global South. This includes creating space for, dismantling barriers to and listening to the perspectives of Brown and Black scholars, leaders, activists and communities in the Global South. This may look like conferences organized by and for researchers / practitioners of color in the Global South; inviting and supporting keynote speeches by scholars, activists and community leaders from the Global South; prioritizing evaluators of color from the Global South to carry out evaluations; appreciating and giving credibility to the rich and diverse Indigenous methods of knowledge generation from communities of color; creating space for and amplifying the voices and leadership of thinkers and activists of color from the Global South and providing safe spaces and resources for evaluators and researchers of color to access peer support, mentorship and other forms of support.

We hope that as our fellow evaluators and researchers in the global development space are becoming increasingly aware of structural racism and neocolonialism in the sector, there is also increasing desire, willingness, and urgency to dismantle the White gaze, obstruct the White Saviour Complex, and reveal and disrupt the underlying White supremacy in evaluation and international development. At the same time, as a sector, we need to surface, expand, build, and strengthen the purposes, values, and practices of evaluation to become truly ethical, respectful, creative, inclusive, and useful in dismantling power structures and inequities.

REFERENCES

Alkin, M.C. (2013) Evaluation Roots: A Wider Perspective of Theorists' Views and Influences, 2nd ed, Los Angeles, SAGE Publications

BetterEvaluation (2020) 'What Is Evaluation?', Global Evaluation Initiative, https://www.betterevaluation.org/en/what-evaluation, accessed 5 November 2021

Cole, T. (2012) 'The White-Savior Industrial Complex', The Atlantic, 21 March, https://www.theatlantic.com/international/archive/2012/03/the-White-savior-industrial-complex/254843/, accessed 5 December 2022

Global Affairs Canada (2016) 'Results-based management for international assistance programming at Global Affairs Canada: A how-to guide. Second Edition', Global Affairs Canada, Ottawa, Canada, https://www.international.gc.ca/world-monde/assets/pdfs/funding-financement/results_based_management-gestion_axee_resultats-guide-en.pdf, accessed 20 March 2022

Kallman, M.E. (2019) 'The "male" privilege of White women, the "White" privilege of Black women, and vulnerability to violence: An intersectional analysis of peace corps workers in host countries', International Feminist Journal of Politics, vol. 21, no. 4:566–94

Kjørholt, T.A. and Penn, H. (eds) (2019) Early Childhood and Development Work: Theories, Policies, and Practices,

Palgrave Studies on Children and Development, London, Palgrave Macmillan

Levin, H.M. (2013) 'Cost-effectiveness evaluation in education', in Alkin, M.C. (ed) Evaluation Roots: A Wider Perspective of Theorists' Views and Influences, New York, SAGE Publications, pp. 180-8

Liverpool, L. (2021) 'Researchers from Global South under-represented in development research', Nature (News), 17 September, https://www.nature.com/articles/d41586-021-02549-9, accessed 18 November 2021

Lorde, A. (1983) The master's tools will never dismantle the master's house. In Moraga, C. and Anzaldua, G. (eds), This Bridge Called my Back. Writings by Radical Women of Color. New York, Kitchen Table Press, pp. 95-101

Pailey, R.N. (2020) 'De-centring the "White Gaze" of development', *Development and Change*, vol. 51, no. 3:729-45

Rees, C.A., Ali, M., Kisenge, R., Ideh, R.C., Sirna, S.J., Britto, C.D., et al (2021) 'Where there is no local author: A network bibliometric analysis of authorship parasitism among research conducted in Sub-Saharan Africa', *BMJ Global Health*, vol. 6, no. 10:1-11

Rivas, A.-M. (2018) 'The everyday practices of development', *Routledge Handbook of Postcolonial Politics*, London, Routledge

SIDA (2007) 'Glossary of Key Terms in Evaluation and Results Based Management: English/Swedish–Swedish/English', Stockholm, Edita Communication

Skoll.org (2021) 'Decolonizing data', YouTube, https://www.youtube.com/watch?v=ue1MEW5Exhc, accessed 17 March 2022

Smith, L.T. (2012) *Decolonizing Methodologies: Research and Indigenous Peoples*, London, New York, Dublin, Zed Books

Stake, B. (2004) 'How far dare an evaluator go toward saving the world?', *American Journal of Evaluation*, vol. 25, no. 1:103-7

UK AID Direct (2019) 'Guidance: Value for money', UK Aid Direct, ukaiddirect.org/wp-content/uploads/2019/06/UK-Aid-Direct-_Guidance-Value-for-Money_June-2019.pdf, accessed 17 March 2022

United Nations Evaluation Group (2020) 'UNEG ethical guidelines for evaluation', UNEG, http://www.unevaluation.org/document/detail/2866, accessed 17 March 2022

Williams, L.G. (2016) 'Ethics in international development evaluation and research: What is the problem, why does it matter and what can we do about it?', *Journal of Development Effectiveness*, vol. 8, no. 4:535-52

3

The Warrior Logic of the White Savior[1]

Leila Benhadjoudja

It's Not Our Tragedy
(Glasser 2021)

It was a heartbreaking sight to see the Taliban take over Kabul in August 2021, just weeks or days from the 20th anniversary of 9/11. Even more tragic were the images of hundreds of Afghans rushing to the Kabul airport, trying to find a seat on a plane. As the United States troops left Afghanistan, many commentators wondered what would happen to the Afghans, especially the Afghan women.

The Western media offered miserable and defeatist reports about the Afghan people, particularly a doomsday spectacle of Afghan women. Very few highlighted the involvement and complicity of the United States' imperialism in the continued violence that Afghans are experiencing. An undertone of this narrative was: But who will save them now? The rhetoric we saw at work in this particular case is not new. The same narrative of 'saving Muslim women' was employed to justify

[1] Several sections in this book chapter are a modified and adapted translation of a chapter published by the same author. See Benhadjoudja (2022).

64

the military invasion of other sovereign countries like Afghanistan, as well as many Western development interventions in the Global South. Like development projects based on this narrative, an invasion like the one of Afghanistan becomes possible by rallying public opinion, where Western imperialism is disguised as an emancipatory discourse for Muslim women.

Another example of the media's negative discourse on Muslim women was the disturbing and controversial photo of Bibi Aysha that appeared on the front page of Time Magazine in 2010. The photo shows this young girl who suffered a violent attack on her face by the Taliban (she had her nose mutilated). In this cover story, Time asked the question, 'What Happens if We Leave Afghanistan?' As many other stories and following the same Western imperialist narrative, the story of Bibi Aysha's suffering has been used as a stage for the United States and its allies to justify the continuation of a war that has deteriorated the lives of Afghan women. Even more, as anthropologist Lila Abu-Lughod points out, 'The controversy over Bibi Aysha indicates how central the question of Afghan women's rights remains to the politics of the War on Terror that, almost from its first days in 2001, has been justified in terms of saving Afghan women' (Abu-Lughod 2013, p. 29).

Just like the photo of Bibi Aysha, the images of the Taliban in Kabul and the scenes of desperation among the Afghan population induce in us the feeling that 'we', as Western powers, have to do something to save them. In other words, in the face of the dangers that Afghan women face, we are driven to support the central figure of Western imperialism: the White Savior.

The 'end' of this war also had a taste of imperialism. After it cost the lives of 47,245 Afghan civilians and thousands of military personnel (Malhas 2021), ironically, the U.S. President

Joe Biden 'lamented the Afghan military and government's lack of "will to fight for [their] future"', (Glasser 2021). The Biden administration's response was to accuse the Afghan military of not knowing how to fight and defend itself. Richard Fontaine, a former foreign-policy adviser to the late Senator John McCain said, 'This is tragic, but it's not our tragedy' (Glasser 2021).

By declaring *It's Not Our Tragedy*, and framing the Afghan army as incompetent, the United States forces are denying responsibility and accountability after more than 20 years of occupation in Afghanistan. This reversal of the situation, in which imperialism places the blame solely on the populations that have suffered from its violence, is emblematic of the colonial and imperial pattern. As the anti-colonial intellectual and psychiatrist Frantz Fanon wrote, 'Colonialism and imperialism are not even with us when they have withdrawn their flags and police forces from our territories. For centuries, the capitalists have behaved in the underdeveloped world as veritable war criminals' (Fanon 2005, p. 103). In other words, after the violence of the imperial and colonial experience, leaving does not end the cycle of violence.

This war, which was waged to strengthen the geopolitical position of the United States in the Middle East under the guise of 'saving Afghan women', is part of a larger project of the White Savior Industrial Complex, which is also present in the field of development (Cole 2012). This project exposes the colonial narrative invented by the West to 'civilize' and justify an enterprise of dispossession, extractivism and exploitation. In this chapter, I adopt a feminist decolonial perspective to critique the figure of the White Savior by specifically analyzing its colonial relationship with Muslim women. To do so, I propose an analysis that considers that by using the 'War on Terror', Western powers present themselves as the saviors of Brown Muslim women (and more specifically Afghan women).

This colonial idea of saving Muslim women is not only present in international politics and relations but also in development aid projects.

I start from the Afghanistan case because it is paradigmatic to show my point: to better understand the rhetoric used during the 'War on Terror' regarding the rescue of Muslim women, it is important to situate it in the broader context of Western colonialism and imperialism. It is relevant to remember that these are the same arguments that justified colonization: by calling the 'Others' undeveloped and uncivilized, the West colonized / plundered / destroyed and presented itself, in a paradoxical gesture, as the savior of what it destroyed.

I focus on highlighting the issue of the coloniality of international relations and the blind spots of the field. Despite the limited critical literature on the subject, aid and cooperation policies have often used old colonial conceptions: those that present the West as a space of emancipation, of human rights advances (of women, LGBTQI2+ and religious minorities), versus the countries of the South (and formerly colonized), as being 'underdeveloped' and in need of aid to reach the path of economic and human development. Maintaining the paradigm of coloniality, the West has given itself a 'moral responsibility' and an obligation to 'help'. This help, in the context of Muslim countries and Muslim subjects in Western societies, goes through the paradoxical movement of waging the 'War on Terror' to save Muslim women from Islam and Muslim men.

THE COLONIALITY OF INTERNATIONAL RELATIONS AND DEVELOPMENT PROGRAMMING

Coloniality is constitutive of 'modernity' and constitutes the foundation of the modern Eurocentric project. Wallerstein (1997) allows us to understand the links between scientific production, the social sciences and the enterprise of Eurocentric domination. According to him, 'Social science emerged in response to European problems, at a point in history when Europe dominated the whole world-system' (p. 93). International relations are marked by this Eurocentrism that poses itself as a mode of knowledge (Capan 2017) and whose analyses are structured by a racism that ignores itself (Zondi 2018). Indeed, this field of study has developed its main concepts, and theorizations from conversations shared among a small group of White Eurodescendant men, whose very conditions of possibility for these conversations rest on imperial violence, colonialism and slavery (*Ibid.*, p. 21). A decolonial perspective claims not only to decenter this single viewpoint but also to highlight the coloniality at work in the narrative that underlies the construction and organization of knowledge in mainstream International Relations.

Embedded in this narrative is the colonial myth that Europeans 'discovered the New World', and that modernity– its political structures, economic and social orientations– would be benefits to humanity that must be forcibly imposed on the rest of the world (Capan 2017). This narrative is punctuated by erasure, absence and epistemic injustices. The otherness found in it makes the other either an object without agency, or, at best, a 'wild' subject to be domesticated, 'dangerous' to be neutralized, or 'poor' to be developed. Zeynep Gulsah Capan (2017) gives a striking example: the erasure of the Haitian Revolution in the historical analysis of international relations, in contrast to the French and American revolutions. The lack of interest and political value given to this revolution is emblematic of the erasure of others and, more specifically, of the racism that structures international relations.

In any case, and this is the main blind spot of international relations and development, coloniality constitutes the foundation of these fields, granting the West the superiority to develop, dominate and theorize over the Other (*Ibid.*, p. 3). Concerning Islam and Muslim populations, the construction of a radical otherness has been built over a long period of time that many decolonial thinkers already refer to as the beginning of European modernity and the Reconquista (Meer 2014, p. 502). This is what also makes Joseph Massad say that Western Non-Governmental Organizations (NGOs) and the entire international human rights community have an orientalist relationship with Muslim countries (Massad 2007, p. 161).

This demonization of Muslims has had a major effect on development policies and the distribution of funds. As many have shown, for example, since 9/11, a large majority of the funds were used to ensure security (especially for NGO workers), understood as a step forward for regional development. Very few funds have been used to actually develop sustainable programs that support the population (Howell and Lind 2009, p. 195). In addition, several analysts have pointed to the political profiling that has resulted in several local Muslim associations being accused of involvement in terrorism without real evidence (*Idem.*).

This is paradigmatically illustrated in the context of Afghanistan and the 'War on Terror'. After Western forces waged war on that country, they then presented themselves as the savior who would develop what they themselves had destroyed. In the specific case of Afghanistan, there were great promises made by the Western coalition to offer aid to develop and rebuild Afghanistan. For example, in 2006, a treaty entitled 'Afghanistan Compact' was signed between the Afghan government, the United Nations and several dozen countries and international organizations. Not only have these promises not been kept but the OECD reported that 25 percent of the aid granted was used for service fees (p. 108).

In addition, a major problem has been the convergence of development policies and military strategies, which has largely sabotaged the work of NGOs in Afghanistan (Howell and Lind 2009). Indeed, the Afghan population was very suspicious of NGO workers. As in other contexts, aid workers (often Westerners and some locals) enjoy a much higher quality of life than Afghans and have very little legitimacy in the eyes of the population. In Afghanistan, many believed that the NGOs were not there to help the Afghans, as reported by an activist, 'They do flagship projects, meaning they put up a big sign saying "gift of the American people" but there is nothing else' (p. 20). Finally, much of the aid, in terms of economic resources and education, did not actually benefit Afghan women, but only those who lived in Kabul, spoke English and had contact with American forces or other foreigners (Fluri 2021).

THE WARRIOR MISSION OF THE WHITE SAVIOR

One of the strong characteristics of the White Savior is this paradoxical movement and duality between making war on one hand and saving on the other. It is this duality that constitutes the main narrative in the Western wars, especially in the Middle East and Afghanistan. However, it is important to stress that war is a central element in the European modernity / coloniality project. Even if the West presents itself as a champion of human rights and peaceful space, its modernity is based on war, which decolonial philosopher Maldonado-Torres (2008) calls 'the paradigm of war'. By this, the decolonial philosopher states that:

the paradigm of war is deeply connected with the production of race and colonialism as well as by the perpetuation, expansion, and transformation of patriarchy. In the modern world, space is mapped as a battlefield principally through colonialism, race, and dehumanizing ways of differentiating genders. War, in turn, is no longer solely found in extraordinary moments of conflict, but rather becomes a central feature of modern life worlds. (p. 4)

Thus, the violence of war initiates and produces colonial differences by leaving its indelible marks on bodies through the politics of race, gender and sexuality. These politics are the grammar of war that is written like a repetitive cycle. By this, we understand that war is not this extraordinary moment that marks history, as the political analyses of world wars claim. In fact, it constitutes the very foundation of modernity. In this paradigm, an ethics of death is played out in a way that naturalizes the death of racialized and colonized bodies. Following the thought of Tzvetan Todorov, who studied the specificities of massacres and violence in the conquest of the so-called Americas, Maldonado-Torres also argues that this paradigm naturalizes the death of racialized and colonized bodies, so that 'massacre, more than sacrifice, is a characteristic feature of modern societies' (*Idem.*).

The "war on terror" is in line with this paradigm. During this war, which began with the invasion of Afghanistan in October 2001, Muslim women played a privileged role in the discourse. Indeed, the Bush administration claimed to be 'saving' Afghan women through the so-called 'just war', thus ensuring public support and the participation of Canadian troops (Thobani 2007, p. 229).

The 'war on terror' thus becomes a staged event, an old colonial ruse performed by three roles: the Muslim, a dangerous terrorist to be neutralized; the Muslim woman, a victim without agency to be saved and the civilized White European man, a savior (Razack 2008). This staging is based on rhetoric at the very foundation of the logic of Eurocentrism and the modernity / coloniality matrix, and which Gayatri Spivak has very well summarized by her now-famous phrase, 'White men are saving brown women from brown men'. Frantz Fanon has also shown that in this colonial staging, the European man maintains a relationship of extreme violence with the Muslim women he claims to save. Fanon qualifies this relation as 'paraneurotic', punctuated by a desire for conquest and possession: 'With the Algerian woman, there is no progressive conquest, reciprocal revelation, but from the outset, with the maximum of violence, possession, rape, quasi-murder' (Fanon 1959, p. 28). In the specific example of French colonization of Algeria, taking over the land is accompanied by violent domination of the bodies of 'Indigenous' women: 'the colonization of land and culture in Algeria was strategically entangled on the body of women such is the articulation of the historical and fantasy' (Yeğenoğlu 1998, p. 65). What Yeğenoğlu highlights is the link between the possession of women's bodies and the possession of land and resources in structuring the logic of colonial and imperial war.

WAGING WAR TO SAVE MUSLIM WOMEN

What is structuring this paradoxical movement of doing war to save Muslim women is the maintenance of the figure of the Muslim as an internal and external enemy and the construction of radical Muslim otherness. In the wake of Said's work on orientalism, many scholars have shown that this otherness is largely informed by racial, gendered and sexual politics and is constitutive of a whole corpus of European philosophy and social science. Through this corpus, Muslim women's bodies become the theatre of colonial fantasy

(Yeğenoğlu 1998), a fantasy fraught with violence and desire for dominance still present in the contemporary era. According to other scholars such as Joseph Massad and Jabir Puar, a similar effort is undertaken for the LGBTQI liberation movement, where there is collusion between a colonial discourse and the gay liberation discourse. According to Joseph Massad, the internationalization of discourses on sexual practices, particularly through human rights organizations, has operated through the colonial and Orientalist paradigms. Thus, international organizations endorsed the idea that not only women but also Arab-Muslim gays should be liberated (Massad 2007).

The objectification of racialized women is fundamental to the warrior mission of the White Savior. This mission must be situated within the framework of colonialism and imperialism, constituting the structuring frames of the relationship between the West and its 'Others.' Both are racial, gendered and sexual projects. As many so-called Third World feminists have shown, colonization was justified by a rationality that claimed to bring European civilization to lands represented as 'savage', 'inferior' and 'barbaric', particularly to 'help' the colonized women (Amos and Parmar 2005, Mohanty 2003). From this point on, we are also invited to understand the connections between White imperialist feminism and the enterprise of colonial domination.

In a seminal book, *The Eloquence of Silence: Algerian Women in Question*, Lazreg (1994) highlights the role that the objectification of Algerian women played in colonial violence. She wrote, 'Through Algerian women, French male writers could satisfy their own desires to penetrate Algerian men's intimate life by having their wives and daughters as spoils of conquest' (Lazreg 2018 [1994], p. 39). Lazreg helps us understand that the silencing of Algerian women works to make them 'consumable'. Being an object of desire and rejection at the same time, they are sexualized in order to better dominate Algerian men. Despite this, these women are always silent and undergo various colonial strategies (hypersexualization and incitement to work in the sex industry, colonial schooling, etc.) to make them indebted to colonial France for their 'liberation' (Chapter 4). This objectification also serves the old sexual stereotypes of Arab-Muslims as having an unbridled, violent, but at the same time, fascinating sexuality. This orientalist sexual apparatus also serves in the mechanisms of the war on terror.

According to Thobani (2014), there is a sexual discourse in the aesthetics of terror. The imprints of this terror on the bodies of Muslim women are often fantasized by what would be the violence of Islam on them: the Islamic veil, the burqa, polygamy, stoning, excision, honor killings, etc. There have been many debates in Europe, especially after 9/11, concerning the wearing of the veil by Muslim women. These debates support colonial arguments that attempt to objectify and control the bodies of Muslim women, forcing them to unveil as proof of their 'emancipation'. This has been particularly the case with the 15 March 2004 law in France and the recent Bill 21 in Quebec, which use secularism to limit Muslim women's civic participation and political autonomy. They operate as an 'anti-political machine', allowing Western societies, on the one hand, to celebrate themselves as progressive (Abu-Lughod 2013, p. 116) and, on the other hand, to maintain the idea that Islam and Muslims would be dangerous for the West.

Thobani (2014) also shows how the sophistication of the aesthetics of terror is illustrated by inscribing the 'monstrosity' of Islam on the bodies of Muslim men. She analyzes how torture in prisons such as Guantanamo or Abu Ghraib was deployed through racial, gender and sexual politics. Several feminist and queer analysts of color have shown that the politics of torture at Abu Ghraib, where photos have circulated in the media, supported the logic of U.S. homonationalism and sexual exceptionalism (Puar 2007). Thobani, in turn, explains that the involvement of White women in this torture served to reaffirm their superiority and complicity in the 'phallic power of the West' (p. 473): 'By breaking Muslim bodies under torture and turning them into a sign of abjection, defilement, and pollution, women maintained the phallic power of the West. It turns out that abjection and monstrosity are focused on the racist politics of the West's sexual dramas' (*Idem.*).

THE WHITE SAVIOR IS ALSO A WHITE WOMAN

Several works by critical race and decolonial feminists have studied the role and function of White women in colonialism and imperialism. They have shown that 'the integration of White women into the institution of White supremacy was critical to the reproduction of colonial relations' (Thobani 2007, p. 170; see also Khan, this volume). In both colonialism and slavery, White women played an active role (Jones-Rogers 2019), which continues to structure the relationship between Western White women and the Global South. This is shown by Chandra Talpade Mohanty in her book *Feminism without Borders Decolonizing Theory, Practicing Solidarity*. In particular, she analyses the work of Western feminists on so-called Third World women and the way in which the latter are homogenized through the discursive category 'women', eternal victims of brown men, their culture and religion. What happens then is the erasure of all political agentivity and subjectivity for racialized women. Through this erasure, Mohanty (2003) argues that Western women set themselves up as norms, as a 'reference', and that this movement also serves to consolidate a set of colonial and imperial techniques. She believes that:

> feminist analyses which perpetrate and sustain the hegemony of the idea of the superiority of the west produce a corresponding set of universal images of the 'third-world woman', images like the veiled woman, the powerful mother, the chaste virgin, the obedient wife, etc. (p. 81)

Mohanty shows that while the 'Third World' was constructed in opposition to the 'First World', the objectification of Third World women also participates in the dichotomies between 'civilized' and 'barbaric', 'White women' and 'racialized women'. From then on, White women of the First World became essential allies for the colonial and imperial enterprises, where they endorsed a pro-war feminist discourse in the name of women's liberation.

Although not visible at first glance in the colonial metaphor of the war on terror, White women play a crucial role here. They perforate the colonial subject by calling for the rescue of women from Islam. Abu-Lughod notes that the mission of some White women to liberate Afghan women is indicative of the former's sense of superiority and is a continuation of the United States' imperialist policy. This policy helps to consolidate 'colonial feminism', on the one hand, and to reaffirm the moral superiority of White women over racialized women, on the other (*Idem.*, pp. 29-53).

Further analysis suggests that 'saving' Muslim women also grants White women privilege in the face of White men's universalist claims to modernity / coloniality. Drawing on the work of Yeğenoğlu (1998), Razack explains that:

> Unveiling the Muslim woman, rendering her body visible and hence knowable and available for possession, renders the Western woman as the colonial, observing, possessing subject. Thus, old colonial technologies enjoy renewed vigour at a time

when Islam versus the West is the hegemonic framing of the New World Order. (2008, p. 86)

Thus, the body of Muslim women embodies the space of competition for possession and the point of access to power in the war paradigm. This body crystallizes the 'paraneurotic' desire that Fanon describes.

Finally, a contemporary example that we can point to that highlights the efforts made by White women to control Muslim women in the name of liberation are the multiple debates surrounding the veil. These debates cross borders and circulate in European countries and Canada in order to caricature the wearing of the veil (or the burqa), and to restrict the freedoms of Muslim women. One example is the secular laws in France and Quebec, where many White women have mobilized in the name of Western feminism (Benhadjoudja 2017, Fernando 2014), resulting in strong political violence against Muslim women (Jahangeer 2020). Yet, unveiling Muslim women in the name of Western moral superiority is an old colonial trick which White women have endorsed. It is the same unveiling to which Egyptian and Algerian women were invited under British and French colonization. The colonial scene that shows a White French woman unveiling a 'native' Muslim woman in Algeria is one that concentrates on the power relations of race, gender and sexuality that colonial domination structures in the name of women's liberation. It is hard not to see how this image resonates with current events and how power dynamics persist even as they take on new forms.

CONCLUSION

The war on terror did not ultimately save Muslim women. On the one hand, it increased violence against them. Also, it destroyed the work done for decades by many local organizations in favor of imperialist feminism supported by NGOization and international development logic (Abu-Lughod 2013). On the other hand, this war consolidated a central element in the logic of war, i.e., keeping the enemy alive through the discourse of terror. This is how the White Savior comes into the picture, they do war in the name of human rights and development. Finally, I tried in this chapter to highlight the links between the war on terror and Islamophobic discourses. I invite readers to see the thread that runs through the circulation of Islamophobic discourses on saving Muslim women across time and space: during colonization, the war on terror or, more recently, through secular laws.

REFERENCES

Abu-Lughod, L. (2013) *Do Muslim Women Need Saving?*, Cambridge, Harvard University Press

Benhadjoudja, L. (2017) 'Laïcité narrative et sécularonationalisme au Québec à l'épreuve de la race, du genre et de la sexualité', *Studies in Religion*, vol. 46, no. 2:272-91

Benhadjoudja, L. (2022) 'Le corps des femmes musulmanes dans le paradigme de guerre', in Sondarjee, M. (ed) *Perspectives féministes en relations internationales: penser le monde autrement*, Montréal, Presses de l'Université de Montréal, pp. 61-67

Capan, Z.G. (2017) 'Decolonising international relations?', *Third World Quarterly*, vol. 38, no. 1:1-15

Fanon, F. (1959) *Sociologie d'une révolution (l'an V de la révolution algérienne)*, Paris, F. Maspero

Fanon, F. (2005) *Les damnés de la terre*, Paris, La Découverte/ Poche

Fernando, M.L. (2014) *The Republic Unsettled: Muslim French and the Contradictions of Secularism*, Durham, NC, Duke University Press

Fluri, J. (2021) 'Reflections on gender and development in Afghanistan 2001-2021', website, University of Colorado Boulder, 9 September, https://www.colorado.edu/geography/2021/09/09/

jennifer-fluri-reflections-gender-and-development-afghanistan-2001-2021, accessed 5 December 2022

Glasser, S.B. (2021) '"Not our tragedy": The Taliban are coming back, and America is still leaving', *The New Yorker*, 12 August, https://www.newyorker.com/news/letter-from-bidens-washington/not-our-tragedy-the-taliban-are-coming-back-and-america-is-still-leaving, accessed 5 December 2022

Howell, J. and Lind, J. (2009) *Counter-Terrorism, Aid, and Civil Society: Before and After the War on Terror*, Houndmills, Basingstoke, Hampshire, Palgrave Macmillan

Jahangeer, R.A. (2020) 'Anti-veiling and the charter of Québec values: "Native testimonials", erasure, and violence against Montreal's Muslim women', *Canadian Journal of Women and the Law*, vol. 32, no. 1:114-39

Jones-Rogers, S.E. (2019) *They Were Her Property: White Women as Slave Owners in the American South*, New Haven, Yale University Press

Lazreg, M. (2018) *The Eloquence of Silence: Algerian Women in Question*, New York, Routledge

Maldonado-Torres, N. (2008) *Against War: Views From the Underside of Modernity*, Durham, Duke University Press

Malhas, M. (2021) 'Afghanistan in 2021: A legacy of American military-industrial nepotism', *Jadaliyya*, 20 September, https://www.jadaliyya.com/Details/43346, accessed 5 December 2022

Massad, J.A. (2007) *Desiring Arabs*, Chicago, University of Chicago Press

Meer, N. (2014) 'Islamophobia and postcolonialism: Continuity, orientalism and Muslim consciousness', *Patterns of Prejudice*, vol. 48, no. 5:500-15

Mohanty, C.T. (2003) *Feminism Without Borders Decolonizing Theory, Practicing Solidarity*, Durham, Duke University Press

Puar, J.K. (2007) *Terrorist Assemblages: Homonationalism in Queer Times*, Durham, Duke University Press

Razack, S. (2008) *Casting Out: The Eviction of Muslims From Western Law and Politics*, Toronto, University of Toronto Press

Thobani, S. (2007) *Exalted Subjects: Studies in the Making of Race and Nation in Canada*, Toronto, University of Toronto Press

Thobani, S. (2014) 'Fighting terror: Race, sex and the monstrosity of Islam', in Suvendrini, P. and Sherene, R. (eds) *At the Limits of Justice: Women of Colour on Terror*, Toronto, University of Toronto Press

Wallerstein, I. (1997) 'Eurocentrism and its avatars: The dilemmas of social science', *Sociological Bulletin*, vol. 46, no. 1:21-39

Yeğenoğlu, M. (1998) *Colonial Fantasies: Towards a Feminist Reading of Orientalism*, Cambridge, Cambridge University Press

Zondi, S. (2018) 'Decolonising international relations and its theory: A critical conceptual meditation', *Politikon*, vol. 45, no. 1:16-31

4

The Matriarchy Complex: White Feminist Disruption in Development

Themrise Khan

The concept of gender and the practices of women's development have been a trademark of the international aid assistance sector for several decades now. Even prior to the 1995 Beijing Declaration and Platform for Action, followed by the United Nations' Millennium Development Goals, both of which institutionally incorporated women's rights into the development sector, women and their lives in the Global South formed a large part of overseas development programming for global aid agencies. Subsequently, gender and women's economic empowerment has become a staple of the Western project and program design in countries of the Global South.

However, as has been the custom in the aid assistance sector, the thrust of this programming has been led by the Global North in most of the Global South. Only women of the South, it is assumed and understood, need to be developed, empowered and given their rights. This attitude has pervaded development since its post-World War Two origins and continues to perpetuate the stereotypes of the poor and needy outside the prosperous and mainly White, Western world of international development. The fact that the word 'international' is also seen as characterizing just the Global South illustrates the myopic tendencies of the Global North in how they view the world around them.

While the White Western male has been the most visible representative of the White Savior in international development as the face of the donor, implementor and manager, his female counterpart has equally perpetuated racist stereotypes. She is the gender 'expert', 'specialist' or 'consultant', who travels from the prosperous North to the underdeveloped South to design, manage, advise or train Southern women (and men), on how to achieve success in gender equality. At a time when gender equality is now as much a topic of discussion in the North as it is in the South, she is also gradually taking over as the face of international development by representing international organizations in the Global South.

While not all Western women can or should be painted with the same brush, many White Western feminists create a power imbalance regarding gender in international development programming. They are the White 'Matriarch'; White women who subconsciously consider their knowledge to be superior to those who belong to other races and, as a result, see themselves as leaders of the tribe. They use their various positions in international development to not just perpetuate White Saviorism but also a matriarchy complex, in which they alone hold the primary position of power over all other women. These White matriarchs of development consider themselves as empowered, independent rights advocates, but only in the context of the Western North, where their experiences are situated. This disconnects them from the realities of the world they choose to work in. For them, feminism is a form of control over women in the Global South rather than a way to bring them together.

In this chapter, I will identify these White matriarchs of development: who they are, how they perceive development and their Southern female counterparts, and what impact this has on gender and women's development as a sector of international cooperation. It will situate this within the wider context and literature on White feminism, colonial feminism and women in development (WID), juxtaposed against 'voices' of women in the Global South and women of color in the Global North about their own views on the White matriarch.

WHITE FEMINISM IN DEVELOPMENT LITERATURE[1]

Mohanty, one of the most prolific critics of White feminism, has consistently claimed that Western WID perpetuates a heritage of White feminism and its assumption that women are a homogeneous group (Mohanty 2003). She famously criticized the application of the 'Western gaze' on women of the Global South by their Northern counterparts, where Southern women are perceived and defined by women of the Global North (Mohanty 1988, 2003).

In a non-development context, it has been the post-colonial and decolonial feminists of the Global South who have laid the basis for many of these critiques.[2] While some have focused

---

[1] The literature review for this section has been conducted by Dr. Maika Sondarjee whose contributions the author wishes to acknowledge and thank.

[2] Established critics of White feminism include bell hooks, Angela Davis, Audre Lorde, Avtar Brah, Gloria Anzaldua, Sylvia Tamale, Maria Mies and Vandana Shiva, Françoise Vergès, Naima Hamrouni, Anna Agathangelou, Meyda Yeğenoğlu, Oyèrónkẹ Oyěwùmí and Maria Lugones.

heavily on discourses and subjectivities (sometimes from an elite standpoint), both have been anchored in the experiences and struggles of everyday women in the Global South. These critiques have often been overlooked by feminists from the Global North, who instead perpetuate the White superiority when referring to women in the Global South. This is particularly the case in international development.

In her study of Whiteness in development aid to the Third World, Goudge notes that Western WID often overlooks imbalances of power between them and the women they want to 'help' (Goudge 2003). Power differentials at various levels, including class, ethnicity, race, citizenship and cultural capital, are often brushed away. She argues that Whiteness establishes the dominance of a particular group of women 'who have the power and the confidence not only to speak, but to speak loudly enough to be heard and be assured of their audience' (Goudge 2003). In this sense, White women assert their confidence to speak above women in the Global South and not just on their behalf.

This mindset has led to a detrimental apprehension and definition of women of the Global South by female development practitioners and academics of the Global North. The former are usually considered as oppressed, underdeveloped and frail, while the latter are perceived as more assertive, free and empowered.

While gender has become a buzzword in aid circles, the Indian feminist and scholar Uma Kothari explains that the 'silence around "race", a term that often does not come into play in feminism, let alone development, allows Western practitioners of development to avoid being accountable for the powers, privileges and inequalities that continue to flow from Whiteness' (Kallman 2019). For example, White WID organizations, she argues, often have 'male' privilege when interacting in countries of the Global South (Kallman 2019).

The victimization of women of the Global South as being weak is not only racialized but also colonial. Various studies of White women activists in colonial Africa and British India have defined the term 'maternal imperialism', which led Western women to frequently refer to themselves as 'mothering' their colonial female subjects (Ramusack 1990, Burton 1992). This matriarchal complex was therefore inherent among White women since colonial times and formed the basis of their attitudes towards their Southern counterparts today.

Likewise, Hamad (2019) writes in her book, *White Tears Brown Scars: How White Feminism Betrays Women of Color* (Hamad 2019) that White women were also colonizers, and their role was equally pivotal to the success of European settler-colonialism, such as the removal of Indigenous children from their families in Australia and the United States. In essence, Anglo-European women themselves bought into the colonial mindset and were far from blameless in the atrocities carried out towards Indigenous groups during the African slave trade.

This 'maternal' or matriarchal mindset of saving the incapable child perpetuated under the scepter of colonization is reproduced in many North–South development projects on the empowerment of women or gender equality. Bandyopadhyay and Patil (2017), for example, analyze volunteer tourism as informed by racialized, gendered and colonial thought. They explain that development actors, especially women, adopt a colonial 'kinship' framework, whereas 'developed, mature' Global North actors help 'underdeveloped, immature' Global South ones (see also Patil

2008).[3]

These insights on colonial relations, maternal imperialism and power hierarchies need to be applied to the development field, particularly in the context of the matriarch. Most research on Western WID and aid organizations has focused on the gendered aspects of their work, their capacity to be respected and the barriers for entry and promotion (Adler 1984, Napier and Taylor 2002, Stroh, Varma, and Valy-Durbin 2000). But very little research has focused on the role of White, Western women in reproducing these colonial, racialized hierarchies in the field of development. As a result, we don't know enough about the White matriarch and what her true motivations are to 'save' or 'mother', women and girls in the Global South. The following section attempts to build a profile never-the-less, based on clichéd existing tropes of the White feminist savior in development.

THE WHITE MATRIARCH IN DEVELOPMENT

In the push to eradicate patriarchy not just in the Global South via international aid assistance–as is the premise of such aid-assisted programs–White women, some willingly, some unwittingly, perpetuate the aura of matriarchy. The historical attitudes described in the previous sections have also fed into this aura of the White matriarch. So, who is the White matriarch in today's development landscape? Altaf (2011) begins her book, *So Much Aid, So Little Development: Stories*

---

[3] Others, such as Kallman (2019), have studied the experience of White and Black women in the Peace Corps, while Syed and Ali (2011) look at White women saviors in the development context.

from Pakistan, with 'Meeting Lucy *memsahib*'.[4] Lucy is a White Canadian 'external consultant' and 'technical expert', recently flown in to work on the Pakistan Government's Social Action Programme by its Canadian donors. The author, who is the 'local consultant' on the project, is, in her own words, forced to 'piggyback' onto Lucy due to the external, Northern donors' funding requirements.

Lucy *memsahib* is suffering from diarrhea and jetlag, seduced by shopping and is mostly oblivious to the state of the social sectors in Pakistan, something the author dreads having to bring her up to speed on. She resides in a five-star hotel, wonders if her clothes are 'appropriate' and, yes, this is her first trip to a Global South country.

This near caricature of a White female development consultant on an aid-induced visit to the Global South may sound farcical, but it is all too often the reality in this field. While the men exude an equally patronizing attitude, the women, like Lucy memsahib, are a mix of both our competitors and our collaborators. Competitors because these women control the positions which should ideally be in the hands of members of the Global South–the country representatives, the project managers, the monitoring and evaluation consultants, the technical experts, etc. Collaborators because in an ideal world as women, we all tend to share a similar history of oppression and neglect, albeit across different cultural and historical contexts.

The White matriarch is not just geographically and professionally separated from her Southern counterparts but

---

[4] *Memsahib* is the colloquial term used to refer to White colonial British women by their Indian 'subjects'. It is connected to the aura of superiority that the British colonists imposed upon the colonized. In post-colonial times, it continues to be used by those of a lower class to refer to women of upper classes.

87

visually as well. She is the lone White woman in a sea of Black or Brown faces, in the absolute center of a group photograph, proudly looking over her flock of participants in a mainstreaming workshop in a country of the Global South. She is the beaming face amongst a sea of children in Africa, Asia or Latin America, having provided them with textbooks. She is the White diplomat looking on from a podium at the inauguration of a women's medical centre or a girls' school, ensuring that everyone knows it was her government that paid for this. She is the lead consultant in the design and implementation of a women's empowerment program, supported by 'local' staff she controls. She is the White academic doing 'field research' in a remote, rural location in a country in the Global South, using a local student to collect her data for her, in most cases, for free.

There are countless more visualizations like this that separate the White matriarch from her surroundings. But the biggest anomaly facing this positioning is that such women do not actually see themselves in this manner. As Francoise Vergès (2021) writes, 'White women do not like to be told they are White ... the feeling of being innocent is at the heart of this inability to see themselves as White and thus protects them from any responsibility in the current world order'.

Even when White women do attempt to perceive and acknowledge their 'otherness', they subconsciously continue to center their own Whiteness rather than take themselves out of the equation altogether. For example, in a special issue of the journal *Gender and Development* on Reimagining International Development, a footnote stated, 'Whilst the conversations were initiated and hosted by a middle-class White woman, based in the United Kingdom, who has worked in the sector for the past two decades, she deliberately endeavored to ensure that a majority were people from Black and Minority Ethnic Groups (BAME) and were located in, and working in, a number of different parts of the world' (Clements and Sweetman 2020). This aspect of 'deliberately endeavouring' to include other Black, Brown and Indigenous women is an indication of both confusion and collusion on the part of White WID to 'give back' the voice of others while continuing to retain their own. These voices were never theirs to take in the first place.

In doing so, not only does the White matriarch ignore the agency of women in the Global South, but she also assumes that she is the only one with the right to view them differently. This has not only created animosity amongst many women development practitioners in the South towards the White matriarch but has also influenced how they view her. The next section highlights some of these views, which receive no space in the discourse amongst female development practitioners.

SOUTHERN VIEWS OF THE WHITE MATRIARCH

While it is clear how White women view their Black, Brown and Indigenous development counterparts in the Global South, with varying levels of superiority and superficiality, how do the latter actually view them? This section amplifies the voices of women from the Global South in various sub-sectors of development, to bring their views into focus.[5] These views highlight consistencies through which the White matriarch undermines the power of women in the Global South. And it begins from a complete awareness on the part of the White matriarch, whether consciously or subconsciously, of her privileged positioning in the development sector. Dr.

---

[5] Some women have chosen to remain anonymous while highlighting their views.

Linda Oucho, a migration scholar and practitioner from Africa states:

> power and positionality of some White Western women who are fully aware of their upper hand use it to dismiss the voices of experts in the field especially if you are a national. They assess you based on the requirements of their institutions in the Global North. I often wonder if we were to do the same thing in their countries as they do in ours, would we receive the same positive reaction or the fact that I am a Black African woman would raise more red flags. Agency is important and when you take that agency from women from developing countries who are already fighting different battles on various fronts, you destroy their motivation and drive.

This shows that reciprocity from the White matriarch remains elusive. Not just in terms of an acknowledgment of the skills, intelligence and capacity of female professionals in the Global South but also in their ability to be critiqued by them. In the mind of the White matriarch, the ability to do that remains in her hands alone, simply because she is White and controls the funding mechanisms. But it is more than just controlling the funding. The White matriarch just does not see the need to engage with her surroundings in any meaningful way. Lazanya Weeks-Richemond (2021), a Black Global health professional originally from the Caribbean, writes in her searing critique entitled 'Dear White Women in International Development':

> As a Black woman in the global health sector who has worked side-by-side with White women for 12 years on public health projects across Africa and the Caribbean, I've found many White women to be culturally illiterate and oblivious to the social nuances involved when leading non-profit organizations and managing projects targeting Black and Brown people. I am perplexed you are genuinely unaware of how to meaningfully engage with the Black and Brown people you work with and on behalf of, or if you are just too lazy to put in the extra effort. The

sector is awash with White Saviors who consistently miss the mark.

Likewise, the presence of the White matriarch in Southern spaces is enough reason for her to usurp the power of women who originally resided in those spaces. An anonymous development activist from South America recalls her experiences of working with such matriarchs:

> There were situations in which without asking a regional group, expenses were paid to someone from the head office to come, someone that only knew the language but had not much to contribute. Her visit was never consulted, it was someone meant to control or supervise what happened in the meeting, as if the history and commitment of the women locally was not reliable enough despite years of work. The [women in the community] could have used the funding for that trip in many ways to support their communal groups, for example, which were in great need of support. I do not mean that these women are evil; it is simply that their experiences make it very hard, for most of them, to understand the realities of women outside their privileged world. They seem sympathetic but with an important degree of condescendence. It seems hard for them to actually treat women of the South on equal basis, in certain areas, especially if these women are not rich or do not come from aristocratic backgrounds.

There seems to be a complete denial of the fact that working in the Global South does not equate to being physically present. This desire to physically control not just the narrative of development but the institutional way of working is what the White matriarch uses to ensure that there is adequate funding for her to transcend her geographical distance from her counterparts. To be successful in her cause, she must actually be there. Therefore, she must always have enough money to be present in the South, even though that money could be spent elsewhere.

But an interesting extrapolation from some Global South development professionals, also veers away from the impact of the White matriarch. They identify the exact same privilege that some Black, Brown and Indigenous women in the Global North exude when they too travel to the Global South. For instance, a Global South researcher who is based in the Global North reflects:

> In my case I find more useful to reflect about my own positionality and how I may oppress others (even if I'm not White), rather than how I may have been 'oppressed' by others, including White women For example, in Latin America, the feminist movement has been criticized for leaving out (or not representing) the struggle of Indigenous women I don't think an Indigenous woman would necessarily feel threatened by a White woman from the so-called Global North who comes to her community with a development or research project–I think she would be more cautious of a woman like me [a Mestiza, with probably higher levels of education, who speaks Spanish]. I think when we think about relationships of power between the Global North and the Global South, we women from the Global South need to also be attentive to our own positionality and how this can materialize when we work with other women from the Global South, because if we are doing development work it's because we are privileged, and we may also be contributing to oppressive relationships in the places where we work that of course are rooted in colonialism but are perpetuated by the dominant society that we are probably part of (in Latin America, the Mestizo society).

This thread of 'reverse' privilege, which turns a Brown or Black woman into a 'White' matriarch, is a fascinating insight into how far perhaps the influence of the power dynamics of the Global North travels. One level of privilege, as stated above, is internal to the dynamics of the South itself, where wealth and class impact relationships between women of the South. Another level is illustrated by Rukhsana Rashid, a development expert from South Asia with three decades of experience working with international aid agencies who describes:

> the 'light skinned / slightly Brown' women who having left their native countries become 'Whiter' than the White women in their new adopted countries. An example is Latino women from different South America nations who migrate at young ages to countries such as Canada. In the adoption of manners, behaviours and social / cultural norms, they actually end up being the Saviors of us Brown and Black women. I found Hispanic / Latino women working at the international aid agency headquarters coming to international postings, mid-career, to be arrogant, and with no sensitivity to local culture. More than that there was little to no respect for the long-standing experience, commitment and hard work of local employees. Often, unfair remarks coupled with a lack of understanding and knowledge led to their quick negative judgmental remarks.

This shows that the impact of the White matriarch on development is not just limited to White women themselves. It also transcends the barriers of race to imbue the elements of superiority, privilege and power in anyone who has had access and exposure to a more privileged life in the North. In effect, the matriarchy complex is not just a racial construct but also a psycho-social one. This impact is explored further in the next section, specifically in the context of the evolution of gender and development in international development over the decades.

IMPACTS ON DEVELOPMENT INTERVENTIONS AND INTERNATIONAL COOPERATION

The evolution of gender and development approaches in international development is a stark illustration of the narrative of control put in place by the Northern aid sector. The Western model of WID was the starting point for all development programming that involved women in the South. It was popularized by the Danish economist Ester Boserup in 1970 based on empirical research conducted in Africa (Aguinaga *et al.*, 2013). Caroline Moser, a White feminist academic from the United States, used these approaches to develop a gender-based model for development programs and projects which differentiated between women's practical and strategic needs, i.e., what they experienced in their day-to-day lives versus what was assumed to be their needs within the larger socio-economic context. This approach was officially adopted by major international multilateral organizations towards all development programming in the South. In reality, Moser's model addressed complex and diverse problems by using an approach that was, in fact, a colonial transfer of Western preconceptions of the inadequacies of the South (*Ibid.*). In essence, academics and practitioners ignored lived experiences of women in the South and, instead, extrapolated onto them an assumed set of needs that did not accurately reflect their realities.

This influenced a Western brand of feminism in development projects, which, as scholars noted, was led by White women who roamed the globe with a mission to rectify the plight of poor women and children (Syed and Ali 2011). Such feminism was markedly different from the feminism espoused by Western philosophers like bell hooks, who saw issues like race equality as the basis for Western feminist thought. Instead, the White matriarch, using the approaches advocated by Moser, interpreted feminism in international development as less an issue of equality between women of the North and South and more of a need to 'help' women in the South attain 'better' lives: better as being defined by the White matriarch, rather than women of the South themselves.

The 'gender expert' became the physical manifestation of the White, Western development feminist. The perfect blend of feminism and development but encapsulated in Whiteness. Indeed, a study that sought to understand the role of gender experts in international development institutions never indicated the racial profile of their over 100 survey respondents in Northern headquarters and field offices. Out of the 21 most influential scholars of gender that influenced the respondents, only four were women of color (and only one was based in the Global South). Likewise, out of the top 20 universities producing the best gender experts, all were in the United States, the United Kingdom and Europe (Thompson and Prügl 2017). This completely negates the idea of both global feminism and global development, where the South has been completely sidelined (Sow 2022, Blackett 2019, Tamale 2020).

This emphasis on Whiteness within the gender and development sector has also had far-reaching consequences in the Global South itself. It has created a corresponding cadre of 'experts', 'consultants' and 'researchers' in gender and development in the Global South, who use Northern methods, knowledge and attitudes to view their own people. This is not only limited to the privileged cadre in the Global South who have the opportunity to study and work in the North but also extends to women across varying levels of class and income in the South who are involved in international development programming vis-a-vis donor or international non-governmental organizations projects. They also perpetuate the myth of power over their female 'beneficiaries', not unlike the White matriarch. Some of the lived experiences contained in this book aptly illustrate this Whiteness that some development practitioners in the Global South mimic.

The manifestation of power perpetuated by Northern aid institutions has also impacted how women in the South perceive not just White matriarchs but also Brown and Black matriarchs who have been brought up in the North. As some of the testimonials in the earlier section illustrate, the view that it is only White Northern women who perpetuate stereotypes also extends to Black, Brown and Indigenous women of the North as well. This negates the assumption that all women who originally belonged to the Global South are in solidarity with each other. The White matriarchy complex is then responsible for conditioning women across a range of racial spectrums to emulate this role, regardless of its appropriateness to their respective personal and professional contexts.

ACHIEVING AUTONOMY FROM THE WHITE MATRIARCH

Following the events of the murder of George Floyd in the United States in 2020, an incident that has ignited an anti-racist dialogue in the development sector, there have been countless calls for White leaders working in global development to dismantle racist and colonial structures. As an analysis of this post-Floyd world claims, this results from the resounding failure of many White self-proclaimed feminists working on gender equality in international development to demonstrate solidarity with the women of color they work with (Women of Colour in Global Development 2021). Almost all the women of color who contributed stories to this analysis were unable to publicly speak up for fear of retaliation by their White female counterparts, most of whom were in senior management positions. Indeed, the analysis itself was written anonymously. This indicates a serious distrust between women of different hues within the Northern aid sector. So one can only imagine the level of distrust between women of the Global North and South.

So how do we rectify this power hierarchy given both its historical connections to colonialism and its current connections to global wealth and the structure and power of Northern development assistance? To start, women of the Global South perhaps have the biggest responsibility to push back against their White Northern counterparts. Their knowledge, capabilities and autonomy mean that any form of development must be designed, managed and run by them and them alone. For the White matriarch, the responsibility lies in stepping back from her perceived role as the 'helper'. In some cases, almost entirely. This would mean refusing to take on any roles that would situate her in a position of power both physically and intellectually in a Southern context.

Instead, she must become an observer and a learner. Instead of imposing her methodology, values and mechanisms of action onto women of the Global South, she must watch from a distance how they impose their own values on themselves. Indeed, this is easier said than done, given the aura of 'sisterhood' and 'solidarity' that White matriarchs also impose and imagine on women of the Global South. They use this as a way of 'bridging the divide'. But what it has done is to erase women of the Global South from the equation altogether.

As Altaf concludes her book, Lucy *memsahib* has fallen in love with the country at the end of her trip and will be back again next month to 'translate the environment' for Sally memsahib, the new head of the United Kingdom's international aid assistance programme in Pakistan, her first posting outside the United Kingdom. The White matriarchy continues, but women in the Global South must not let it.

REFERENCES

Adler, N. (1984) 'Women do not want international careers: And other myths about international management', *Organizational Dynamics*, vol. 13, no. 2:66-79

Aguinaga, M., Lang, M., Mokrani, D. and Santilla, A. (2013) 'Development Critiques and Alternatives: A Feminist Perspective', in Lang, M. and Dunia, M. (eds) *Beyond Development. Alternative Visions From Latin America*, Amsterdam, Rosa Luxemburg Stiftung, Transnational Institute

Altaf, S.W. (2011) *So Much Aid, So Little Development. Stories From Pakistan*, Baltimore, Johns Hopkins University Press

Bandyopadhyay, R. and Vrushali, P. (2017) '"The White woman's burden"–The racialized, gendered politics of volunteer tourism', *Tourism Geographies*, vol. 19, no. 4:644-57

Blackett, A. (2019) Everyday *Transgressions: Domestic Workers' Transnational Challenge to International Labor Law*, Ithaca, Cornell University Press, ILR Press

Burton, A.M. (1992) 'The White woman's burden. British feminists and "the Indian woman"', in Chaudhuri, N. and Strobel, M. (eds) *Western Women and Imperialism: Complicity and Resistance*, Bloomington, Indiana University Press

Clements, M.A. and Sweetman, C. (2020) 'Introduction: Reimagining international development, *Gender & Development*, vol. 28, no. 1:1-9

Goudge, P. (2003) *The Power of Whiteness: Racism in Third World Development and Aid*, London, Lawrence & Wishart

Hamad, R. (2019) *White Tears Brown Scars. How White Feminism Betrays Women of Colour*, Melbourne University Publishing

Kallman, M.E. (2019) 'The "male" privilege of White women, the "White" privilege of Black women, and vulnerability to violence: An intersectional analysis of peace corps workers in host countries', *International Feminist Journal of Politics*, vol. 21, no. 4:566-94

Mohanty, C.T. (2003) *Feminism Without Borders: Decolonizing Theory, Practicing Solidarity*, Durham, Duke University Press

Napier, N.K. and Taylor, S. (2002) 'Experiences of women professionals abroad: Comparisons across Japan, China and Turkey', *International Journal of Human Resource Management*, vol. 13, no. 5:837-51

Patil, V. (2008) *Negotiating Decolonization in the United Nations: Politics of Space, Identity, and International Community*, New York, Routledge

Ramusack, B.N. (1990) 'Cultural missionaries, maternal imperialists, feminist allies: British women activists in India, 1865-1945', *Women Studies International Forum*, vol. 13, no. 4:309-21

Sow, F. (2022) 'Mobiliser les femmes dans l'Afrique contemporaine', in Sondarjee, M. (ed) *Perspectives féministes en relations internationales*, Montreal, Presses de l'Université de Montréal, pp.71-80

Stroh, L.K., Varma, A. and Valy-Durbin, S.J. (2000) 'Why are women left at home: Are they unwilling to go on international assignments?', *Journal of World Business*, vol. 35, no. 3:241-55

Syed, J. and Faiza, A. (2011) 'The White woman's burden: From colonial "civilisation" to Third World "development"', *Third World Quarterly*, vol. 32, no. 2:349-36

Thomson, H. and Prügl, E. (2017) 'Gender experts in international governance: Mapping the contours of a field', in Verschuur, C. (ed) *Expertes en genre et connaissances féministes sur le développement: Qui sait?*, Geneva, Graduate Institute Publications

Tamale, S. (2020) *Decolonization and Afro-Feminism*, Ottawa, Daraja Press

Vergès, A. (2021) *A Decolonial Feminism*, London, Pluto Press

Women of Colour in Global Development (2021) 'The limits of feminist solidarity', *The Medium*, 31 March, https://woc123.medium.com/the-limits-of-feminist-solidarity-328f1589d420, accessed 18 November 2021

5

False Consciousness and the Phenomenology of White Saviorism

Kanakulya Dickson

Two works provide a backdrop to this discussion, i.e., *The White Man's Burden* (Kipling 1899) and *Heart of Darkness* (Conrad 1899). The former was a poem that called on the United States to colonize the Philippine Islands and civilize them. The latter was a novel that used fictional characters to explore the darkness (immoral behavior) either brought to or found in Congo by the White man. This raises the question: Does 'darkness' exist in a geographical location, or does it exist in the hearts of the Europeans who invaded Africa? It was ironic that in the same year, one White person was calling for more White Saviorism while the other was passing an indictment on its darkness.

Recent efforts towards the decolonization of development theory and practice have taken interest in the phenomenon of the "White Savior Complex' or White Saviorism within the development aid industry (Bex and Craps 2012, Cole 2012, New African 2015, Fisher 2016). There is a need to investigate the moral questions that arise from the White Saviorism implicit in this sub-field of development. White Saviorism is one of the perennial underbelly moral challenges in the global development aid industry, especially in the African context.

This chapter uses the framework of 'false consciousness' to interrogate the ethical implications of White Saviorism in development. It develops a philosophical diagnostic with the concept of false consciousness to answer the fundamental questions of the White Saviorism within the development industry.

Although there is a conception of false consciousness in terms of class struggle, this chapter applies the understanding of false consciousness provided by Lewis Gordon as 'bad faith' and 'moral decadence' (1995). Gordon explores this understanding at the psychosocial level of analysis. He defines bad faith as the attitude in which human beings attempt to evade freedom and responsibility, which results in practices that involve the construction of other people as fundamentally inferior and sub-humans. This, psychologically, results in a pleasing falsehood that creates a consciousness of the deceived. It is a form of narcissistic existence whereby the racist, who is otherwise a human being like any other, presents himself as superior precisely because he lies to himself and is, therefore, in bad faith. He deceives himself that he is superior, and this belief is self-justifying because he believes in it. The racist does not feel or think that his beliefs need justifying; it is enough that he believes in them and gives a stability of self, a sensation of superiority (Kiros 2008). He calls this condition 'malignant narcissism', which forces negative and false images of the self onto others and a preoccupation with fantasies about success, power and brilliance.

INVENTING THE WHITE SAVIOR

Like much of the world, which assumes that 'White' people have a divine assignment to spread 'superior morals' around the world, the historian Conklin Alice inadvertently promoted the same assumption in her book *Mission to Civilize* (1997). Despite her criticism of the French for their failure in their colonial 'mission to civilize' Africa, it seems like she only disagreed with the method rather than the 'mission'. In her criticism, the French had failed to transfer their republican ideas of the 'rights of men' from liberal France to the African colonies because of the desire to economically exploit the colonies. Similarly, William Easterly's scorn for the failure of development aid in his book *The White Man's Burden* (2006a) does not investigate the fundamental question of why White people feel the need to carry the 'White man's burden'. Easterly's rebuttal of similar criticism of his views generically blamed institutional failures and bureaucratic behavior within global aid organizations, such as the United Nations and World Bank (Easterly 2006b). Nonetheless, he makes an insightful observation by mentioning corruption as one of the reasons why poverty persists in countries receiving aid because it ' block[s] opportunities for poor people to solve their own problems ' (*Ibid.*). By mentioning corruption, Easterly is indicating that the problem is moral in nature. It should be noted, however, that when he is referring to poor countries, he calls it 'corruption', but when he is referring to the United Nations and World Bank, he states that they ' have virtually no accountability'. The problem is the same in poor countries, and in the international Western-based aid organizations, i.e., they are morally wanting. For that matter, this chapter approaches international development as a White endeavor, which requires critical development analysis to unravel the undercurrents of its perennial challenges.

The word 'savior' in the phrase White Savior'requires more philosophical analysis because it is the gist of the moral problems resulting from the enterprise of White Saviorism. Commenting on scandalous 'saviorism', David Jefferess (2021) has observed the danger of 'the continuing normalization of saviorism as an orientation that naturalizes philanthropic or charitable approaches to alleviating suffering as both just and effective' (Jefferess 2021, p. 420). Jefferess' concerns indicate that when the White Savior is weighed on the scale of the self-assigned mission of global development 'salvation', there is a lot that is found wanting. The appendage of 'savior' to 'White' is an elevation of almost divine proportions, rendering the rest of the people in need as lesser beings. It is certainly doomed to fail the 'just and effective' test because of a pedestal too divine to be or reach.

The 'savior' terminology is a superlative word that goes beyond assistant and helper. For there to be a 'savior', there must be one who needs to be 'saved' and from conditions that require a 'savior's intervention'. In theological terms, we know that the 'savior' intervenes from another dimension that is superior in terms of morality and knowledge. The 'savior' performs the eternal miracle of salvation upon the needy helpless lesser beings out of mercy. But the savior's moral compass has to be beyond reproach to qualify for being the savior. The 'mission' and the 'being' of the savior must be profoundly connected for the sacrifice to be divine. In discussing the recently exposed morally wrong practices within the WE Charity organization in Canada, Jefferess raised the mischievousness of the tendency to separate between the original 'righteous path' of a White Savior organization and the 'wrong practices', which prop up later. In other words, even though many 'saviors' White elephant organizations and projects have resulted in moral scandal after moral scandal, there seems to remain the view that the 'original' mission of being a savior is a good idea and a 'righteous path'. The desire to maintain White Saviorism as a good ideal to aspire to is problematic in itself. It attracts many would-be saviors in different shapes and colors, thus perpetuating the moral problems within development theory and practice.

MORALITY AND FAILURES IN DEVELOPMENT AID

Thinkers like Goulet (1971) and Gasper (2008) have long argued that the underlying problem in the development industry is moral in nature. This implies that the perennial failures and ills in the development industry are fundamentally a result of moral inconsistencies. They define development ethics as a field that examines the ethical and value questions related to development theory, planning and practice (Goulet 2008). Development ethics is a field of inquiry that reflects on both the ends and the means of economic development and focuses on the inequalities and relationships within the development world. Gasper argues that this field raises normative perspectives that ought to guide development trajectories and engages in the discourse on ethical, fair and just implementation of development policies and projects. He proposes that development ethics has four main perspectives, namely a) comparative, b) dynamic, c) intercultural, and d) international.

The saviorism within development discourse is rooted in moral views of development aid. In 1996, Opeskin relied on the moral principles of distributive justice, corrective justice and humanitarianism to argue for increasing development aid to states in need (Opeskin 1996). Tomohisa Hattori used the Aristotelian perspective of virtue ethics to argue that foreign aid should be viewed as a moral issue. He argued that foreign aid between nations should go beyond reciprocal relations between states into a form of 'multilateral beneficence' among states (Hattori 2003, p. 297). However, by the 1950s, thinkers were already warning about the moral challenges involved in foreign aid. The World Council of Churches observed that 'most far-reaching and intractable problems which the various programs of foreign assistance face do not lie in the technical but rather in the moral and ethical realms' (World Council of Churches and Bilheimer 1957, p. 1).

The field of development ethics has made considerable progress. Still, less than necessary attention has been given to examining the question of personal moral agency in development theory and practice. A big segment of the development industry is occupied by charity workers and volunteers, and this sub-industry relies on individual moral agency and self-regulation. It is assumed that as such, charity organizations receive donations and the funds put to use by morally upright and accountable personnel. Unfortunately, stories of misbehavior and patronizing saviorism abound from the field of development. Bandura (2002) has argued that moral agency has dual aspects, i.e., a) the power to refrain from behaving inhumanely and b) the proactive power to behave humanely. Moral agency is embedded in a broader socio-cognitive self-theory encompassing affective self-regulatory mechanisms (*Ibid.*). But there is a need to centralize the moral questions implicit in any development aid agenda.

It is true that Non-Governmental Organizations (NGOs) fill a crucial gap in development that was a result of colonial failures. But we must ask ourselves if there is an inherent problem in using the aid approach in development practice. Has transforming from 'charity' to 'industry' affected the development aid approach? Colonial powers had no desire to finance state welfare programs for colonized Africans. Government social services for the Indigenous population were minimal. Social policy was geared towards ensuring the integrity of the structures of colonial rule with very little attention or resources allocated to the natives (Manji and

O'Coill 2002). Because of this gap, NGOs became part of the 'development machine' in formerly colonized countries. This 'development machine' is a vast institutional and disciplinary nexus of agencies, practitioners, consultants, scholars and other miscellaneous experts producing and consuming knowledge about the developing world (*Ibid.*). International development has become a big business. By 2020, the OECD countries reported that Official Direct Aid to other parts of the world had reached $118 billion, with 70% of this aid in form of humanitarian aid.

There is also growing discomfort with the White Saviorism expressed as international foreign aid. The Zambian economist Dambisa Moyo, in her book, *Dead Aid* (2009), showed the futility of using Western foreign aid to develop the economies of poor countries. She argued that as foreign aid has increased over time, Africa's growth has decreased with an accompanying higher incidence of poverty. In 60 years, over $1 trillion had been 'sent' to Africa, but there was nothing much to show for it. She concludes that Africa does not need aid but mutual trade opportunities and the opening up of international markets by the so-called donor countries. Although Moyo is currently working in the private corporate sector, it does not diminish the strengthened and enduring relevance of her argument, which should make us rethink the aid industry. The fact that the aid industry has increased still with meager results to show may be indicative of the fact that this aid is benefiting other parties rather than the intended 'beneficiaries'. The 2015 report on Illicit Financial Flows from Africa further cemented the growing view that foreign aid is not the answer for developing countries, especially in Africa. The report found that Africa loses over $50 billion annually through illegally earned funds that are transferred by international corporations. This is an indication of the significant moral failure of the international business community in Africa. What Africa and other less developed countries need is to stop these illegal practices and allow fair trade globally.

One of the reasons why international development aid is being called into question is because, despite the vast sums invested in aid, there is little to show for what it has done over the years. Despite many accountability failures and inhuman behavioural scandals reported among aid workers and charity organizations, huge amounts of funds are still being raised for humanitarian aid. Perhaps, the continuation of the donations both by the state and individuals indicates a genuine by misinformed desire to 'save the other' (particularly in the Global South). This sounds more like a morally questionable situation that requires closer inquiry.

MORAL FAILURE OF WHITE SAVIORISM IN INTERNATIONAL DEVELOPMENT

The development aid industry has a history of White Saviorism, which still casts a shadow of the colonial 'White man's burden' mindset. Attitudes of White Saviors are still perpetuated at both macro and micro levels of the international aid industry. The White Savior industrial complex is built on centuries of imperialism and reductionist imaginary solutions to problems of people battling colonial legacies (Kagumire 2020). In his article on 'The White Savior Industrial Complex', Teju Cole argues that the smaller savior efforts are part of larger disasters behind them, i.e., the militarization of poorer countries, short-sighted agricultural policies, resource extraction, the propping up of corrupt governments and the astonishing complexity of long-running violent conflicts over a wide and varied terrain (Cole 2012).

Discussing the moral failures of White Saviorism in international development has to consider two segments of analysis, namely the moral and the geographical. In terms of the former, White Saviorism needs to be examined for the unending moral scandals that keep showing up to establish whether it is an institutional or personal responsibility. The latter looks at the geographical dimension of White Saviorism to establish whether it is only practiced outside the White Savior's country or not.

In discussing the case of the Canadian WE Charity, Jefferess (2021) reported that investigators exposed rampant selfish financial malpractices within the organization that benefitted the managers. After being exposed for the rampant questionable financial dealings, structural racism and abusive behavior, WE's co-founders, Craig and Marc Kielburger, 'announced plans to change WE's governance structure and refocus its energy on international development work ' (p. 421). The reported decision by the WE co-founders is indicative of the roots of the moral failures of White Saviorism at the level of international development. Why does the Canadian White Savior of questionable moral character find it more comfortable to operate in other countries at the international level?

Perhaps such conduct further explains how White Saviorism takes the rest of the world for granted, being the self-assigned 'saviors' they can operate all around the world and get away with almost all moral questionable behavior. There are several reports of the moral failure of White Saviors at the global level ranging from big international organizations to small community organizations in poor countries. A few years ago, despicable reports of Oxfam workers sexually abusing and exploiting women and girls in Haiti surfaced, shocking the world. It was observed that 'Privileged White men giving devastated, impoverished women of color money for sex is vile exploitation, not prostitution' (Moore 2018). Moore posits that abuse comes from power imbalance and 'happens in places where those caring for the powerless break the implicit trust. In care homes, boarding schools and religious institutions, all these places that operate in their own unique moral universes, the most vulnerable have been abused by their so-called protectors' (*Ibid*.). In 2018, several international NGOs, including prominent ones like World Vision, were expelled from Indonesia by the government, ordering all foreign aid workers to leave because of the mess they had made of the rescue efforts after a tsunami-triggered earthquake devastated the country. The government stated that those organizations were hampering the rescue and recovery work (Kate 2018).

The moral failure of White Saviorism in international development is also found in small organizations that are scattered across the world in less developed countries. Apart from the failures of the big international organizations, countless low-level incidents have been reported of purported 'White Saviors' taking advantage and abusing the needy that they claimed to be assisting. For example, there was the case of Beery Glaser, a German health professional who arrived in Kalangala islands (part of the remote Ssese islands in Lake Victoria) in 2003 as a tourist and a social worker internee. Later, he started an NGO called Ssese Humanitarian Services. A few years after, investigators found that he was sexually abusing the young girls in his care home and recording pornographic materials which he would sell on the dark web for financial gain. He ended up being sued in court for gross illegal sexual misconduct and sexual exploitation of the children but died of cancer before the case was disposed of (URN 2019). Another case of moral failure was that of Renee

Bach, an American missionary who moved to Jinja, Uganda, at age 18 and started an NGO called Serving His Children. It is reported that with no formal medical training, Renee Bach started experiments of complicated medical procedures on children under her care, which she would search and learn from YouTube. This led to the death of over 100 children. She tried to settle the case by paying off the grieving mothers, but an activist group, No White Saviors, is demanding accountability for the lost lives; therefore, the case was still in court at the time of this publication (McCool 2021).

MORAL AGENCY AND WHITE SAVIORISM

Current international development aid theory pays little attention to the question of personal moral responsibility in international development practice. Most likely, this is due to the heavy reliance on sentimental resource mobilization (mostly religious guilt driven). There is evidence to show that a sizable segment of persons that donate to charity organizations do so out of a sense of induced guilt created using effective marketing tools. Basil *et al.* (2008) studied this phenomenon. They established that induced guilt creates a sense of empathy and self-efficacy which determines behavior and results in maladaptive responses to donating. This results in a weak or ineffective development aid accountability culture, which fails to ask questions of personal moral character. The examination of moral agency and of, ethical responsibility and accountability in the international development aid industry is quite weak. Despite the numerous moral scandals and questionable practices that have been reported by researchers and the media about these 'White Saviors', there is little to no accountability shouldered by them. They continue with their work as if these things are not happening.

To examine the question of accountability, we have to look at the issue of moral agency to establish the moral state within White Saviorism. Moral agency is understood as the ability to make ethical decisions about what is right or wrong. This ability can be exercised by either individuals or collective entities. A moral agent should normally have the capability to discern right from wrong and can be held accountable for their own actions. Most moral theorists think that rational beings (self-interested) are the ones capable of moral judgments and, therefore, can be considered moral agents. Determinist moralists believe that human actions are the results of antecedent causes. But such a position would be incompatible with free will because it exonerates the one who acts wrongly, claiming that humans have no real control over their actions. We must, as a matter of necessity, believe in free will because the ethical fabric of society is founded on this belief, if not then all ethical and legal institutions would collapse. Rational beings are considered moral agents capable of making right or wrong decisions and liable to being held accountable when they decide or act wrongly. For that matter, those who raise themselves to a high moral pedestal have to be held accountable for a higher moral behavior.

The capacity for rationality was considered a preserve of 'White' colonizers at the height of colonialism, with some prominent thinkers such as Immanuel Kant arguing that colonized people were incapable of rationality (Kant 2004). They suggested that colonized natives had limited rationality and lacked basic moral capabilities. However, other thinkers disagree with the erroneous view that colonized people, such as Africans, lacked the capacity for 'rationality' (Chukwudi 1997, 2008). Chukwudi studied the original notes of Kant's lectures in anthropology and discovered that Kant believed and taught that non-Europeans lacked 'reason' because nature did not give such people (i.e., Africans and Red Indians) the 'gift' of rationality (Chukwudi 1997, p. 115). This view was perhaps borrowed from social Darwinism, which was a dominant sociological theory, but it reduces non-Europeans to the state of less than humans hence justifying the mistreatment and immoral behavior of colonialists around the world. However, this is a wrong belief because, according to Chukwudi, rationality is a capacity that all humans have (Chukwudi 2008). Likewise, Scanlon (1998) argued that 'reasoning' is not limited to certain people because all communities have the capacity for 'good reasons' and shared moral behavior (Scanlon 1998, p. 153).

This also means that the moral agency of the White Savior is not beyond accountability, and neither is his rationality superior to the needy persons being assisted. Instead, the capability to discern right from wrong of the White Savior who commits gross moral misconduct is adversely affected by certain conditions that require investigation. In her phenomenological study of how White people develop a critical consciousness of White Saviorism, Willer-Kjerbaoui identified five stages which they undergo, i.e., socialization, dissonance, distance and performance, introspection and reconstruction (Willer-Kjerbaoui 2019). One of the values of Willer-Kjerbaoui's study is that it examines White Saviorism from a phenomenological point, and it also examines it as an issue of consciousness. In terms of the first stage of socialization, Willer-Kjerbaoui questioned the production of White Savior narratives in current popular media. However, White fragility often hinders White individuals' ability to listen to and value other perspectives (p. 6). This explanation can hold water to the extent that a historical and global analysis is not involved. Still, when we consider history and events worldwide, we easily notice that 'White fragility' has not been

112

blocking Europeans from realizing their moral misconduct. White Saviorism has been going on for as far back as history can inform us. We, therefore, need to go beyond the surface psychological blame of 'White fragility' to establish what the deeper roots of immoral White Saviorism are. I think understanding the nature of consciousness that informs White Saviorism should help answer many questions about the morality therein.

FALSE CONSCIOUSNESS AND WHITE SAVIORS BURDEN'

Consciousness provides us with an appropriate avenue to interrogate the moral issues resulting from the White Savior Complex within development practice. It enables investigation into the question of moral responsibility and agency. This is done using the concepts of 'false consciousness' and 'bad faith' as espoused by the philosopher Lewis Gordon. He argues that 'bad faith' motivates racist choices and thus undermines the true freedom of the racist (see: Bart, 2008:51; Kiros, 2008:138; Lewis, 1995). White Saviorism is, by extension, a globalized form of racism disguised as assistance to the needy. What makes it a matter of consciousness is the fact that today many new persons working in such organizations in the Global South are enacting a White Saviorism attitude. This has affected not only the young generation of former colonial powers but also secondary actors worldwide.

The 'false consciousness' explicates the phenomenon of an individual unwittingly taking on the persona of a White Savior. Lewis Gordon posits that for an individual to personify racism, they must adopt a false consciousness of artificial superiority despite their lived experiences proving otherwise (Lewis, 1995:95; Kiros, 2008:138). Gordon's view implies that if you are such as individual you face It is a constant inner struggle to keep convincing yourself that you are a 'savior' and the other is a lesser human who needs your salvation. The White Savior faces an inner existential threat to her artificial persona of 'savior'; she knows internally that she doesn't measure up to the actual requirements of a real 'savior,' but she must keep up the appearance, as it were. This means that the actual nature of the burden is not the 'White man's burden' but the White Saviors burden'. In the case of Renee Bach, she had to rely on YouTube videos to pretend to be a medical doctor. The White Savior must do everything to appear a savior to her needy victims. This means that there is ground to hold the 'savior' accountable for the personal consciousness that has been internally nurtured into abusive actions that negatively affect the development agency.

As a result, the White Savior pretends to function at a higher moral plane or within a moral void or a non-human moral continuum which provides a snowballing effect into moral decadence. The 'savior' has to be the brave immortal that travels to 'difficult' parts of the world among barbaric and uncivilized lesser mortals. This is translated by the White Savior as a licence to run roughshod over any moral limitation placed by society on human conduct. The 'savior' feels that she has earned the right to make decisions and make up their own moral rules on the go. Any consideration or evaluation of the work of the 'savior' ignores concerns over moral responsibility.

Therefore, four main characteristics can be observed in the White Saviors burden'. The first one is the failure to extricate oneself from the morally corrupt colonial legacy and vestiges; the White Savior shows little interest in outrightly condemning the evil that was done during the colonization process and she enjoys the illicit praise former colonial masters accord to themselves. It is, therefore, not surprising that most White

Savior moral scandals are committed by individuals from former colonial countries. The second one is that White Saviorism involves self-congratulations both as a way to silence the internally repulsive moral contradictions on the savior's conscience and to project an image of inner satisfaction on the outside. This is a result of the moral echo-chamber within which the White Savior operates. The third one is that White Saviorism has to necessarily make dogmatic religion its ally because religious favour and sentimentality ensure weak accountability mechanisms that lack the requisite moral rigor for international development. The last observation is that White Saviorism relies heavily on a morally reductionist view of complex development issues.

CONCLUSION

The attitudes of White Saviors are still perpetuated at both macro and micro levels of the aid industry. However, if international development practice is to lead to sustainable development around the world, it must necessarily be built on a strong moral foundation (Kanakulya 2015). Development requires ethics on which it can be founded; efforts not founded on good ethics ultimately become untenable and short-lived. They lack the requisite integrity, humaneness and justice to enhance the lives of the persons being assisted. A viable ethical fabric in society ensures the realization of development sustainability and the realization of sustainable development systems and processes.

REFERENCES

Bandura, A. (2002) 'Selective moral disengagement in the exercise of moral agency', *Journal of Moral Education*, vol. 31, no. 2:101-119

Basil, D.Z., Ridgway, N.M. and Basil, M.D. (2008) 'Guilt and giving: A process model of empathy and efficacy', *Psychology & Marketing*, vol. 25, no. 1:1-23

Bex, S. and Craps, S. (2016) 'Humanitarianism, testimony, and the White Savior industrial complex: What is the what versus Kony 2012', *Cultural Critique*, vol. 92:32-56

Chukwudi, E.E. (1997) 'The color of reason: The idea of "race" in Kant's anthropology', in Chukwudi, E.E. (ed) *Postcolonial African Philosophy: A Critical Reader*, Oxford, UK, Blackwell Publishers Ltd

Chukwudi, E.E. (2008) *On Reason: Rationality in a World of Cultural Conflict and Racism*, Durham, NC, Duke University Press

Cole, T. (2012) 'The White-Savior industrial complex', *The Atlantic*, 21 March 2012

Conklin, A. (1997) *Mission to Civilize: The Republican Idea of Empire in France and West Africa, 1895-1930*, Redwood, CA, Stanford University Press

Conrad, J. (1899) 'Heart of darkness', *Blackwood's Magazine*, London, UK

Moyo, D. (2009) *Dead Aid: Why Aid Is Not Working and How There Is a Better Way for Africa*, New York City, NY, Farrar, Straus and Giroux

de Haan, A. (2009) *How the Aid Industry Works: An Introduction to International Development*, West Hartford, Connecticut Kumarian Press

Easterly, W. (2006a) *The White Man's Burden: Why the West's Efforts to Aid the Rest Have Done So Much Ill and So Little Good*, London, UK, Penguin Books

Easterly, W. (2006b) 'The White man's burden', *The Lancet*, vol. 367:2060

Fisher, T. (2016) 'Challenging the White-Savior industrial complex', *The Plan Journal*, vol. 1, no. 2:139-151

Gordon, L.R. (1995) *Bad Faith and Antiblack Racism*, St. Anthony, ID, Humanity Books

Hattori, T. (2003) 'The moral politics of foreign aid', *Review of International Studies,* vol. 29, no. 2:229-47

Jefferess, D. (2021) 'On Saviors and Saviorism: Lessons from the #Wescandal', *Globalisation, Societies and Education*, vol. 19, no. 4:420-31

Kanakulya, D. (2015) *Governance and Development of the East African Community: The Ethical Sustainability Framework*, Linkoping, Linköping University, Department of Culture and Communication

Kant, I. (2004) *Observations on the Feeling of the Beautiful and Sublime*, Trans. by John T. Goldthwait, Oakland, CA, University of California Press

Kiros, T. (2008) 'An essay on the evolution of Lewis Gordon's thought: From bad faith to disciplinary decadence', *The CLR James Journal*, vol. 14, no. 1:138-50

Manji, F. and O'Coill, C. (2002) 'The missionary position: NGOs and development in Africa', *International Affairs*, vol. 78, no. 3:567-83

McCool, A. (2021) 'US missionary faces new legal action over child deaths at Uganda Health Centre', *The Guardian*, 20 January

Moore, S. (2018) 'The Oxfam scandal shows colonialism is alive and well', *The Guardian*, 12 February

New African (2015) 'Inside the White Savior industrial complex', *New African Magazine*, 6 January

Scanlon, T.M. (1998) *What We Owe to Each Other*, Cambridge, MA, Harvard University Press

URN (2019) 'Suspected German pedophile now ready to plead guilty', *Observer*, 11 June

Willer-Kjerbaoui, J. (2019) *Working Through the Smog: How White Individuals Develop Critical Consciousness of White Saviorism*, North Andover, MA, Merrimack College

World Council of Churches, and Robert, S.B. (1957) 'Ethical problems of foreign aid and technical assistance', *Aluka*, https://bit.ly/3ga2uwV, accessed 10 August 2021

6

Epistemological Underpinnings and Emancipatory Insights on White Saviorism in Development

Kizito Michael George

The term development etymologically stems from the Latin word *veloper* (wrap up), which, when combined with the prefix 'de', means to unwrap from within. The root of the concept development is, therefore, indicative of the endogenous nature of ethical development. Such development must derive from internal epistemologies, resources, capabilities and endowments. Exogenous development initiatives should only come in to empower internal development efforts from within. This implies that they should not alienate and denigrate endogenous development resources.

White Saviorism perverts the motive and nature of ethical development by maligning endogenous epistemologies and resources as backward, inferior and uncivilized. This consequently leads to the control and colonization of development in a way that favours the Global North, which cheaply appropriates resources from the Global South (Bandyopadhyay 2019). Therefore, behind the White Savior Complex (White Savior Complex) are deeply knitted

118

epistemologies and discourses of power that define and situate the supposed truth about development. In other words, what we know about development, how we know it and how we justify it are socially constructed to validate the White Savior Complex.

This chapter explores the hidden epistemological distortions embedded in development theories that motivate humanitarian assistance and development practice. It confronts the tendency to fundamentally associate the White Savior Complex with development practice or humanitarian assistance. The chapter argues that the White Savior Complex is more visible and possibly more forceful in humanitarian assistance. However, it is reinforced and concretized from a theoretical level. This is actualized through the implicit and explicit inculcation of opinions, attitudes, perceptions, biases, distortions, disinformation and misinformation about development, poverty and well-being, right from childhood to adulthood. I advocate for painstaking emancipatory criticisms of Global North epistemologies to realize the implementation of emancipatory development practice.

SOCIALIZATION AND WHITE SAVIORISM

White Saviorism is based on structural racism that fundamentally aims at the dehumanization and subjugation of people of color. The victims and villains of White Saviorism are socialized into accepting it through deeply entrenched social structures that impose covert knowledge bases that create hardened perceptions in the minds of the objects and subjects of the White Savior Complex.

The White Savior Complex is reinforced during both primary and secondary socialization. Primary socialization occurs within the home setting of both nuclear and extended family structures and is inculcated by mothers, fathers,

119

guardians, elder siblings, grandfathers and grandmothers. At this level of socialization, White, Black and Brown children are equipped with informal theories about Whiteness. These beliefs subconsciously create hardened perceptions about the benevolence of White people towards Black and Brown people, which influence these people as they progress to mature stages of decision-making.

These informal theories are derived through watching movies, films, news, documentaries and cartoons about White people saving Africans, Asians and Latinos from war, crime, poverty, hunger, disease, earthquakes, and tornadoes, among other vagaries. People of color are depicted in films, movies, media and government statistics as criminals, prostitutes, serial murderers and kidnappers who need White people to save them from themselves. Examples of films with a White Savior genre are 'Glory (1989), Dangerous Minds (1996), Finding Forrester (2000), The Last Samurai (2003), Freedom Writers (2007), Avatar (2009), The Blind Side (2009) and The Help (2011)' (Hughey, 2015). They are further crystallized through talking to and listening to conversations with adults about White superiority and civility, which are often juxtaposed with Black, Asian and Latino backwardness, savagery and inferiority.

The White Savior Complex is further enhanced at the secondary level of socialization, which takes place in schools, churches, social clubs, social media, national and international civil society organizations and the internet, among other centers. At this level, adults are primarily socialized through formal theories about the White Savior Complex. However, socialization through informal theories is still very much evident even at this stage. For example, covert theories are propagated at this level by constructing Jesus Christ, the Savior of mankind, as a White person. This evokes the covert theory that without Whites, people of color cannot attain salvation from sin, death and hell. Another example is evident in teaching Black children during a history lesson that a White man discovered a lake on which Africans had been fishing for hundreds of years before the arrival of the White man. Overt knowledge bases inculcated during secondary socialization are evident in modernization theory, basic needs theory, trickle-down approaches and neoliberalism. According to modernization theory, for instance, African societies are still backward because they have not embraced science and an industrial ethic. The traditional sector in most African societies needs to be dismantled to pave way for modernization. It must be noted that White Saviorism is premised on the zeal to modernize traditional and backward Black and Brown societies so that they catch up with civilized Western societies. Overt theories are primarily imparted to people through the primary, secondary and tertiary school systems.

ENDOGENIZATION OF DEVELOPMENT PROBLEMS AND EXOGENIZATION OF SOLUTIONS

The White Savior Complex is premised on a false narrative that blames development problems in the South on domestic causes such as dictatorship, corruption and bad governance. This endogenic thesis is oblivious to the global structural injustices that produce and reproduce poverty in developing countries in the Global South. Of course, poverty is partly caused by domestic factors such as patriarchy and other forms of gender injustice; however, poverty in Africa, Asia and South America is fundamentally caused by global structural injustices such as the austerity measures embedded in structural adjustment programs that have been imposed on these states through colonial institutions.

It is therefore paradoxical that several White Savior Complex-oriented humanitarian workers come to Africa every year to solve what they believe to be exclusively domestically caused development problems, such as lack of drinking water, lack of electricity, hunger, poor healthcare, poor sanitation and poor education. These problems are fundamentally propelled by White Savior Complex development theories like neoliberalism. Neoliberal macro-economists through the World Bank and the International Monetary Fund have, for instance, urged African governments not to prioritize giving the poor social amenities like water, electricity and agricultural subsidies using the argument that this will stifle economic growth. According to neoliberal approaches, water, health and food are not rights but aspirations that the poor will futuristically enjoy as economic growth improves.

As a result, several developing countries in Africa and Asia have promoted privatized access to water and electricity, which are expensive, while completely ignoring the affordability of these two amenities. Consequently, many poor people in these countries, especially in villages and slums, are drinking dirty water. In contrast, expensive clean piped water from government corporations or private firms flows right beside their residential premises. In addition, although electric poles are located adjacent to their dwellings and sometimes right in their compounds, some poor use unhygienic kerosene lamps and candles because electric power is unaffordable to them.

THE PROJECTION OF AFRICAN NATIONS AS
FAILED STATES AND WESTERN ONES AS MODELS

In December 2012, the United States National Intelligence Council projected that 10 out of 15 countries that risk being failed states in 2030 are from the African Continent. These states are Somalia, Burundi, Uganda, Malawi, Democratic Republic of Congo, Kenya, Niger, Nigeria, Chad and Ethiopia (National Intelligence Council 2012). A close scrutiny of these countries reveals that these states have all previously been advised to implement structural adjustment programs. These neoliberal austerity measures have been ardently supported by the World Bank, the International Monetary Fund and the U.S. Treasury (Washington D.C.-based institutions). It must be emphasized that neoliberal policies on the African continent have bred dictatorships, poverty, kleptocracy, corruption and fraud (Wiegratz 2019).

Wiegratz argues that:

> 'global capitalism has never been more advanced and aggressive than now. A key feature of this intensively global capitalist world is the staggering level, variety and institutionalization of fraud and other economic crimes, across economic sectors. Wherever you look, the extensive societal restructuring of the last 30 years, that is 'neoliberalism', has produced structures and conditions that are fraud-enabling. Corporate power and profit-making are closely tied to theft, deception and lawbreaking, in oil, mining, manufacturing, retailing, accounting, banking, education and health' (*Ibid.*, p. 357).

Whyte and Wiegratz (2016) reiterate that 'fraud is not merely an epiphenomenon but is a core feature of the structure of neoliberal capitalism' (p. 6). For instance, although the right to health is a backbone of economic development because development pre-supposes a sound population in terms of health and well-being, austere neoliberal structural adjustment programs obliterated the health sector in several African countries by imposing a reduction in state spending (Gatwire *et al.*, 2020). The right to adequate health has been turned into a prerogative for rich and middle-class Africans. Consequently, health facilities have become very expensive for the poor, who comprise the majority population in Sub-Saharan Africa.

Neoliberal states in Africa were lured by the World Bank and International Monetary Fund to desist from investing in high-quality drugs and medical treatments in government health facilities (Ichoku and Ifelunini 2017). Many rich elites and politicians with heart disease, kidney failure and other complicated ailments are flown out of the country to be treated in expensive medical facilities. At the same time, the poor with similar illnesses are left to suffer with no assistance. The sick nature of many health systems led some members of the academia to become nostalgic about the state of public hospitals and medical facilities during colonialism.

In addition, using the incredulous argument that the market will solve all problems in the development process, many neoliberal African states have paid minimal or no attention to food reserves (silos) and agricultural subsidies for peasant farmers. The provision of agricultural subsidies is considered to be injurious to economic growth and development, according to neoliberalism. This is a clear deviation from the stance of Pan-Africanists like Julius Nyerere and Kenneth Kaunda, who looked at food reserves and agricultural subsidies as so central to their full-belly thesis.[1] The neglect and privatization of food reserves and agricultural subsidies have not only impoverished millions of Africans but also rendered thousands of Africans malnourished and undernourished amidst plenty of food.

---

[1] This thesis is premised on the thinking that economic and social rights like the right to adequate food take precedence over civil and political rights such as the right to vote. In other words, the right to vote is meaningless if you have an empty stomach (hungry).

The International Monetary Fund, the World Bank and the U.S. Treasury, are largely responsible for failing African states. They have advised the above 10 states on the verge of failure to fundamentally focus on economic growth instead of social welfare priorities. Consequently, social rights such as health, education and electricity have been privatized and are unaffordable for the poor (Abouharb and Cingranelli 2007). More so, a number of youth in Africa are unemployed. This has created social despair, hence leading to violent social disobedience against the states (*Ibid.*).

MODERNIZATION AND EPISTEMOLOGICAL
AUTHORITARIANISM IN DEVELOPMENT

The White Savior Complex in international development is characterized by both epistemological (cognitive) and ontological injustice. The former subordinates alternative views of the world (de Sousa Santos 2016) that are not in tandem with Western positivist perspectives, and the latter 'subordinates and excludes not just "alternative views of the world", but "views of alternative worlds"' (Wilson 2017, p. 1083).

Ontological injustice means that 'it is not just that the worlds are different, but that they are differently and unequally valued. It is not simply that we must acknowledge that different people view the world differently, but rather that we must be open to the possibility that different people inhabit different worlds' (*Ibid.*, p. 1083, para. 25). In other words, there are different ways of living in the world (Wichterich 2014).

For a long time, Africans have been told by White Saviors that the only way to develop is through modernization. This simply means moving away from rudimentary means of production to scientific means and hence industrialization. Development has meant progression from primitive states to industrialization. Developed countries in the West have all followed this trend, and developing countries must follow suit.

With the prominence of the climate change debate, Africans are tacitly being told to go slow on modernization and industrialization due to anthropogenic global warming (AGW). AGW is the theory that humans are responsible for the emissions of carbons that are claimed to be causing global warming. African states see this as an unethical and unjust move to curtail their right to development and their desire to catch up with the West. They are convinced that developmentalism is the way to go.

The epistemic injustice against Africans in international development has conditioned leaders into the deception that modernization and the emulation of Western states is the way to go, even when it is achieved at the expense of planetary health. Views from Africa on development have been treated by Western institutions as implausible and untenable. The White Saviorism, which is explicit in international development, has forced Africans to understand themselves using Western concepts and paradigms. This has created hardened colonial perceptions about development that are inimical to environmental and climate justice.

NEOLIBERAL SCIENTISM AND
ETHICS-LESS DEVELOPMENTALISM

The neoliberal ideology is premised on a positivist outlook, which envisages development as a scientific process governed by market forces. This process is oblivious to ethics, human rights and social justice. This, in principle, means that the responsibility for underdevelopment and maldevelopment rests on the market and not the state. According to the neoliberal perspective, the state must refrain from undertaking ethics-oriented development prescriptions, such as greening the economy, degrowth and climate change mitigation.

Neoliberal modernization has perplexed African states to immense proportions. African leaders have been lured to make a paradigm shift from a fixation with modernization to a preoccupation with market-oriented neoliberal prescriptions. These leaders have been de-schooled from fixing democracy, human rights and social justice to fixing markets, GDP and, consequently, economic growth.

Neoliberalism has deceptively conditioned African leaders into thinking that science will fix all that pertains to development and human well-being. Despite the global hullabaloo about the global climate change crisis, many African leaders see climate change activists as trick stars who are destructing them from their goal of catching up with the West. African states still strongly believe that modernization is development and development is modernization. They are ready to embrace technology, industrialization and urbanization to catch up with the West, even if this is attained at the expense of environmental degradation.

FLAWS IN THE CONCEPTUALIZATION OF
WHITE SAVIORISM IN DEVELOPMENT

A criticism of the White Savior Complex is not an argument to evict White persons from African development or development of the South. Human development-oriented partnerships, engagements and interventions between the North and South or between the Western and developing world are very healthy and should be encouraged. But they are being premised on human development, implying that they do not treat Black and Brown people as objects of development but rather as equal participants in the development process. These kinds of partnerships are difficult to find, but they ought to be promoted and protected.

Development interventions that are not embedded in the White Savior Complex are premised on dialogue and not on the superimposition of development perspectives from the Western world. They ought to aim at empowering Black and Brown people to be at the center of their development and should be based on the highest level of participation, which is also known as empowerment.

Although many White people might be looked at as villains behind the White Savior Complex, they are actually also victims of the White Saviorism narrative and mentality. For instance, White Saviors working in humanitarian assistance (volunteer tourism) are motivated by a socialized desire to help others and a refusal to listen to guidance from those they want to help. They believe that they must lead and never follow because they are better than the people they are helping (Flaherty, 2016).

Black, White and Brown people are objects of the White Savior Complex in the sense that they are used as cogs in perpetuating the complex. However, unlike Black and Brown people, Whites are subjects of the White Savior Complex because this paradigm aims at entrenching and safeguarding White privilege and White supremacy. Empowerment of all races to confront and eliminate the White Savior Complex is therefore necessary for providing a critical mass against the White Savior Complex.

Willer-Kherbaoui argues that White Saviorism, as a form of individual, cultural, and institutional racism, results in the systemic silencing and dehumanization of Brown and Black individuals by maintaining White privilege while simultaneously upholding systems of oppression' (Willer-Kherbaoui 2019, p. 4). He also opines that 'one step that can be taken to work toward eliminating White Saviorism is to support White individuals in becoming more effective in their racial justice efforts, particularly with regard to changing the structures and systems upholding current power imbalances' (Ibid.). Willer-Kherbaoui further argues that in order to deconstruct mentalities, narratives and systems that construct White people as saviors, and Black and Brown communities as objects of the service, there is a need to develop a critical consciousness against the evils of White Saviorism. He surmises that eliminating White Saviorism requires a critical engagement and confrontation of 'the individual, cultural, institutional, and systemic levels of racism' (Ibid., p. 50).

CONCLUSION

The White Savior Complex is a racist stereotype entrenched through both covert and overt epistemological strategies that produce and reproduce the White Savior Complex through both primary and secondary socialization. The White Savior Complex is premised on injustices that fundamentally inculcate epistemicide against Black and Brown paradigms and discourses on international development. There is, therefore, an urgent need to occupy international development through critical engagement and advocacy for the implementation of emancipatory knowledge bases. The critical pedagogies embedded in the emancipatory knowledge projects will be vital in de-socializing, de-colonizing, mobilizing and empowering White subjects and Black and Brown objects of White Saviorism to transit into a critical mass of vicegerents against it.

REFERENCES

Abouharb, M.R. and Cingranelli, D. (2007) *Human Rights and Structural Adjustment*, Cambridge, Cambridge University Press

Bandyopadhyay, R. (2019) 'Volunteer tourism and "the White man's burden": Globalization of suffering, White Savior complex, religion and modernity', *Journal of Sustainable Tourism*, vol. 27, no. 3:327-343

de Sousa Santos, B. (2016) *Epistemologies of the South: Justice Against Epistemicide*, New York, Routledge

Flaherty, J. (2016) *No More Heroes: Grassroots Challenges to the Savior Mentality*, Edinburgh, AK Press

Hughey, M. (2015) 'The Whiteness of Oscar Night', *Contexts*, 19 January, https://contexts.org/blog/the-Whiteness-of-oscar-night/, accessed 15 August 2021

Ichoku, H. and Ifelunini, I. (2017) 'The changing political under currents in health services delivery in Sub-Saharan Africa', *International Journal of Health Services*, vol. 47, no. 3:489-503

United States National Intelligence Council (2012) 'Global trends 2030: Alternative worlds. A publication of the National Intelligence Council', National Government Publication, https://www.dni.gov/files/documents/GlobalTrends_2030.pdf, accessed 28 June 2021

Whyte, D. and Wiegratz, J. (eds) (2016) *Neo-Liberalism and the Moral Economy of Fraud*, Abingdon, Routledge

Wichterich, C. (2014) 'Occupy development–Towards a caring economy', *Development*, vol. 56, no. 3:347-49

Wiegratz, J. (2019) '"They're all in it together': The social production of fraud in capitalist Africa', *Review of African Political Economy*, vol. 46, no. 161:357-68

Willer-Kherbaoui, J. (2019) 'Working through the smog: How White individuals develop critical consciousness of White Saviorism', *Community Engagement Student Work*, vol. 29:1-63

Wilson, E.K. (2017) '"Power differences" and "the power of difference": The dominance of secularism as ontological injustice', *Globalizations*, vol. 14, no. 7:1076-1093

7

Imposition and Reproduction of White Saviorism in Haiti

Rose Esther Sincimat Fleurant[1]

Analyses of international development cooperation in Haiti highly question its effectiveness. Numerous studies point to its inconsistency, its unilateral character and its failure (Seitenfus 2020). However, the main international 'development' agencies and national institutions continue to hang on to it. The state refers to it in all its public policies as a major and unavoidable strategy. No decision on the management of the country's political affairs is effective without their authorization. This justifies to a large extent that development cooperation serves the interests of the dominant Western actors rather than the Haitian population.

These foreign stakeholders, who believe themselves to be benevolent, exercise constant decision-making influence on all socio-economic, socio-educational, cultural, environmental and other policies. They consider themselves unrepentant lecturers, and this tendency is accepted in both public and private institutions, political structures and associations.

---

[1] Translated from French

Indeed, this willing posture twists the multiple national reconstruction efforts.

The organization of actions conceived in such a context progressively impoverishes the Haitian nation and dictates to it with the most brutal ferocity, attitudes and behaviors modeled on a White Savior prototype. The objective of this chapter is to examine the process of construction and implementation of this model of thought and its pre-eminence in development cooperation in Haiti. I will also indicate certain strategies that can help deconstruct it.

THE CONSENTING SOCIAL CONSTRUCTION
OF THE WHITE SAVIOR

Very soon after its independence, on 1 January 1804, the Republic of Haiti resounded itself under the grip of its former colonizers. The latter's stranglehold on its cultural resources, and more particularly, its spirituality, slowed down its vigorous and creative impulses and its determination to organize and build its institutions. This imperialist attempt to dispossess it of its identity through fierce repression has manifested itself in the imposition of White supremacy (DiAngelo 2020).

Thus, the country is obliged to choose the references and the vision of its colonizer. In opposition to its emancipatory thought, it subscribes to a set of social attributes based on the devaluation of the know-how and the knowledge-of-being of its inhabitants. And to regain control, France demanded the payment of an indemnity of 150 million gold francs, renegotiated to 90 million, for the recognition of its independence acquired by the bravery and intelligence of its slaves. This sum is valued today at more than $40 billion. What morally repugnant behaviour was displayed through this debasing compensation? However, at that time, the Haitian authorities let themselves be chained. What ineptitude. The totalitarian domination started there on the right foot.

It turns out that the freedom of the slaves in Santo Domingo was a prejudice.

By accepting this terrifying order in 1825, Haiti closed itself up in the petrified shell of its former invader and became a consenting subordinate. It fell back on its knees before its commanders and proclaimed its unwavering allegiance to them. The origin of its current poverty is undoubtedly located in this bloody exploit of its master. A little later, in 1915, the United States came to corroborate the White ferocity (Plumelle-Uribe 2001) by its ruthless occupation.

Thereby, a crisis of self-recognition occurs between a critical mass of citizens who continue to fight for their freedom and dignity and an elite that promotes neo-colonial values. Today, subjugation completely permeates the thinking of the Haitian population. The de facto White protectorate, a state dominated and controlled by a nation that considers itself more powerful, as is the case with Haiti's political reality, is a posture rooted in the management and administration practices of the country's political and public affairs. The governors and the governed hold on to the Western powers, loving their lessons. They constantly solicit their imposing presence even if they pretend to take a certain distance.

The political, economic and intellectual elites (Casimir 2009) refuse to act without the permission of Western actors. The ideology of a White messiah takes hold of their knowledge and consciousness. This ideology is the basis on which the institutions and organized structures of society plan and execute their activities. In reality, the way in which the 'elites' act and behave demonstrates their slavish attachment to the vision of the Western powers. A form of co-constructed agreement around these 'White Saviors' is established and remains unchanged. To safeguard their multiple socio-economic and political interests, they invent all kinds of mechanisms, methods and techniques of action and interaction to the detriment of the mass population. And, faced with the resistance of certain categories of actors to their macabre games, they reinvent strategies depending on the context.

FORMAL INTERNALIZATION OF WHITE SAVIORISM

Haitian society is marked by a hostage-taking of its identity. The educational system imposed by the new oppressors in complicity with the 'national elites' conveys images of submission, dependence, unworthiness, etc. Formal education highlights illustrations, facts, stories and models that project the supremacy of a Western way of thinking.

Teaching is a space of shaping, conscientization and reproduction. The school as a place of learning portrays a symbolic 'White'[2] character gifted with an unparalleled intelligence that must be adored. It uses repetition as its main teaching technique and leaves no room for reflection and inventiveness. The students' reflexivity is stifled by the constant profusion of representations of this messiah to whom everything must be expected and before whom one must prostrate.

---

[2] Marie Charlène told me one day that her school is doing very well following the appointment of two foreign professionals (White man/White woman): an administrator and a pedagogical manager. When I asked him what the objective was, he said that many more parents are coming to enroll their children and the school has gained a great reputation. The parents are meeting the deadlines, and the bursar's office is doing well. People just have to know that White people are on the management team so they value everything that is done. I can't complain, everything is running smoothly now.

This misrepresentation shapes the content of the formal and informal learning process in educational, social and political institutions. The church and the mass media reinforce this model. Therefore, the brainwashing of everyone remains constant, regardless of their background. The denial of one's identity as a Haitian has reached its peak. In this sense, a new spirituality that is entirely consistent with the desires of Western powers is being arranged into a value system that establishes the absolute authority of the 'White man'.

The educational institutions, as they are conceived, their practices of organization and transmission of knowledge, remain a means of mass destruction of the Haitian people. Receiving an education does not offer Haitians the possibility of guaranteeing their well-being, recognizing their rights, appropriating their culture and accepting and assuming themselves. In fact, the educational institutions function according to the wishes of the dominating powers that control the school system. The prioritized teaching methods disconnect the learners from the realities that surround them, from their language and from their deep spirituality centred on the national cultural referents. Ultimately, they lead them to hate themselves and constantly want them to behave like submissive children, modern-day slaves. This process leads to the rejection of the national identity and the destruction of the country's capacity to negotiate and intervene as an interlocutor. It offers no possibility of engaging in cooperation.

This suggests that the extermination of the cultural identity of the Haitian people by their White oppressors forces them to hang on to them and do their bidding. In addition, the predatory national oligarchs, who have taken up the cause of these neo-colons, skilfully ensure the process of total alienation (Fanon 1967) of the nation. They present themselves as local decision-makers and influence all internal decisions.

Considered as local representatives of the oppressors, they manipulate everything to force the population and its leaders to adopt *restavèk*, that is, 'domestic' attitudes and behaviours, by someone who carries out the orders of his master or mistress.

PUBLIC INSTITUTIONS AS
INSTRUMENTS OF DEPENDENCY

The White Saviorism ideology is well-established in Haitian institutions. It is expressed through measures and intervention programs. Generally, institutional practices are based on imported experiences (Providence 2020) that obscure the national reality. White paternalism prevails in public structures and in the mechanisms of reflection and action.

The unquestioning docility to the concerns of the international oligarchy considered as so-called partners remains visible. The types of domination are well assimilated by the institutions both in their organization and in the execution of their routine and emergency activities. The so-called international development agencies influence all national actions. They legitimize their authority and power by establishing memoranda of understanding in which they grant themselves all the rights and all the authorities and impose slavish obedience on national institutional actors. A consenting administrative domination is built.

All national structures function under the sway of foreign powers that ensure the design, planning, coordination, monitoring and evaluation of their programs. In reality, the steering of activities in the areas of public security, justice, environment, health, education, agriculture, etc., is experimenting with the techniques and approaches of these Western laboratories. The state decision-makers pretend to work in synergy when they simply execute the so-called development policies designed and developed by the international institutions.

The knowledge, experience and recommendations of local experts are valued if and only if foreign experts approve them. Their contribution is often overshadowed by their own. The exchanges that took place during the elaboration of the strategic plan for the development of Haiti, the health policy and the gender equality policy remain obvious references.

If it is useful to consider the contributions of specialists from abroad, it is not undeniable to underline their dominating behavior (see Gutierrez and Gilbert 2019). At different levels, these 'specialists' consider themselves entitled to decide the fate of Haiti and want to prescribe their strict and deterministic rules. Their relays at the national level also adopt this same posture. If we look at the facts, establishing any form of cooperation with a dependent country like Haiti appears completely incongruous.

On many occasions (workshops, multi-sector meetings, etc.), the attitudes of both Haitian women and foreign women also demonstrate that the perception of the 'White man' as 'supreme leader' and 'savior' is a reality. During a meeting at the Hotel Montana in March 2016 on the promotion of women's rights, Noman Narseaud and Sernora Irema Annie, two international executives, demanded the presentation of the latest report on the Convention on the Elimination of All Forms of Discrimination against Women (CEDAW). The authorities present, without worrying about the time of preparation or about who would do it, gave a positive response. Whispers spread all over the room: some people think that it is necessary to do it quickly, this request cannot be postponed; otherwise, it will be a bad note. Others apologized for not having included this item in the agenda, stating that it was a mistake. The room was somehow silenced by this demand. Most of the participants used all types of flattery to please these two executives, delegates. They must not get angry; otherwise, the consequences will be too great. However, two weeks before the activity, Sanite Lajoie, a civil servant, had demonstrated the importance of dealing with this point. Lajoie was excluded from the organizing team. At the end of the day, everyone was scrambling for souvenir photos with the international representatives. This is important, as the size of the meeting depends on it. This state of mind shows us how much the White Savior ideology is instilled in society.

Institutions such as the Prime Minister's office and its organs, the Provisional Electoral Council, the ministries and their autonomous agencies let themselves be subjugated. It is not uncommon to find in these public institutions consultants recruited as part of a 'partnership', who decide on the policies and programs to be implemented. These experts reject the work done by managers and trivialize their experiences to arrogantly dictate their own instruments and strategies. One of the most obvious cases is that of Caswina Granjan. This national expert on the promotion of women's rights had to face institutional interference of proximity during a working session on the establishment of the sub-cluster on gender-based violence (GBV) in 2010. A group of 'international' experts ordered the formation of a new national structure to fight against violence against women and girls (GBV sub-cluster) at the expense of the national consultation, which represents the national mechanism to fight against it.

This group pointed out that this was a measure and not a proposal. Granjan's statement was the following: 'I am not here to negotiate a decision, but rather to study the mechanisms of its implementation, the sub-clause is applied everywhere, you have to get to work'. With this decision, she

139

overturned with a backhand all the work of the National Round Table on Violence against Women, which has been in place for more than six years and has proven its worth. This certainly caused some discontent, but everything was quickly back in order. The 'White man' decided that's okay. This affair allowed us to understand not only the effects of neo-colonialism in the weakening of institutions but also the degree of submission that is established there. What is most surprising is the enthusiasm for apologizing for what was said. Moreover, the fashionable formula: 'he found his White man', he has the power and the authority to act and to make people act.

The expression 'S/he has his White man' is synonymous with s/he has his savior. He can open all the doors and can, make decisions and influence all actions. He is an irresistible liberator, a true facilitator. *Depi m gen yon blan avèm, m tout bon* (it is enough for me to have a White man with me for everything to work out) or with the presence of a White man by my side everything will work out, that is how it is with us. Besides, the 'White' is in everything. His decision is expected to act when it is not simply imposed. Everyone wants to be close to the White man, to have him in their album or in their activity. The White Savior participates largely in the fabrication of social imaginary, which needs to be deconstructed.

The 'authorities' comfort themselves in these labor interference practices. They blindly implement all their decisions and attest that it is the White people who set the tone. Even if they have to face some institutional resistance, they look for their own White Savior as soon as they take office to implement joint programs that can help them ensure their visibility. In this game of dominant and dominated stakeholders, cooperation struggles to play its role, and institutions deviate from their mandate by prioritizing the objectives of international powers.

DECOLONIZATION OF DEVELOPMENT COOPERATION

The White Savior is part of the Haitian collective imagination and has become the norm. If it is to be deconstructed, it is essential to decolonize the school, the church and the mass media. The school environment must install a new spirituality centered on dignity, freedom, pride, and the construction of social, moral and aesthetic human values. It is this basic priority approach that can gradually lead to the eradication of sheep-like attitudes and behavior in international negotiations.

Broadly, it is a matter of rethinking the educational system and making social institutional spaces to express Haitian culture and its symbols. This requires the development of new strategies necessary to de-alienate the brains of the population, the rulers and the elites. Based on the principle that a colonized state cannot have a government capable of positioning itself as a potential partner, it is essential to rethink it. The adoption of such a provision proves the willingness of national actors to build cooperation that respects the rights and dignity of the Haitian people. This work requires a societal rupture.

Without the re-appropriation of the Haitian identity and the reformatting of the brain of the elites, development cooperation can only remain an instrument at the service of Western powers. Self-recognition as a citizen cultivating a sense of commitment to one's homeland becomes a major issue. Better centralized perspectives on the valorization of the Creole language, of the national culture, deserve to be defined by the institutions. This is what can stop the phenomenon of acculturation, which strips the nation of its existence and buries it.

All these elements of change converge towards the creation of a new social dynamic in which the elites, national leaders and colonial empires feel the need to morally redefine themselves. Development cooperation can no longer be accepted as an instrument to reconquer former colonies. Decision-makers must learn to say NO to foreign powers that want to keep the country in the most abject subjugation. It also forces neocolonizers to recognize the dehumanizing consequences of their new forms of invasion and to banish from their practices any tendency towards White spiritual supremacy (Thuram 2020). The deconstruction of the posture of *restavèk*, 'domesticity', of slavish obedience remains one of the determining factors in the process of annihilation of the thinking based on the apprehension of the 'White' phenomenon as 'savior'.

The reformatting of the collective consciousness is indispensable, and the resocialization of individuals a necessity. Generally, the country's institutions, promoters of the practices of consenting domination on which the society is organized, must be rethought and decolonized. The reorganization of society is a decisive way to acquire the necessary capacities to build structured, efficient and loyal cooperation.

REFERENCES

Casimir, J. (2009) *Haiti et ses élites: l'interminable dialogue de sourds*, Port-Au-Prince, Éditions de l'Université d'État d'Haïti

DiAngelo, R. (2020) *White Fragility: This Racism That Whites Do Not See*, Paris, Les Arènes éditions

Fanon, F. (1967) *Black Skin, White Masks*, New York, Grove Press

Gutierrez, G.S. and Gilbert, R. (eds) (2019) *Cooperación internacional en Haití: tensiones y lecciones: Los casos de Brasil, Chile y México*, Mexico City, Instituto Mora Publishers

Plumelle-Uribe, R.A. (2001) *La férocité blanche: des non-blancs aux non-Aryens, génocides occultés de 1942 à nos jours*, Paris, Albin Michel

Providence, C. (2020) 'Development aid in Haiti: Paradoxical responses to territorial imbalances', *Nouvelles perspectives en sciences sociales*, vol. 16, no. 1:181-216

Seitenfus, R. (2020) *International Dilemmas and Failures*, Sao Paulo, Alameda Casa Editorial

Thuram, L. (2020) *La Pensée Blanche*, Mexico City, Philippe Rey

8

The White Saviorism, Corporate Sector and Land Rights in Central Uganda

Robert Kakuru

White Saviorism is a common view that sees White people as saviors of other social groups (Sturges 2015, p. 117). It is a false form of generosity, which preserves and symbolizes White supremacy by framing White foreigners as heroes and other groups as unable to help themselves (*Ibid.*). White Saviorism is also known as the White Savior Industrial Complex, 'a confluence of practices, processes and institutions that exemplifies the historical inequality of the eventual establishment of White privilege' (Anderson 2013, p. 39). For this reason, people are incentivized to 'saving' the unlucky and unsuccessful and may ignore the policies that create and maintain the oppressive regimes that they support. Western countries often refer to less-developed nations as chaotic, war-prone and blood-thirsty and position them as places in need of saviors. This mentality glorifies the need for outside powers to intervene and salvage the situation. However, what stands out from this conversation are the roles that those outside powers played, through colonialism and White supremacy, in creating these conditions. As Dearden (2017) states:

> 'Africa is poor, but we can try to help its people is a simple statement, repeated through a thousand images, newspaper stories and charity appeals each year, so that it takes on the weight of truth. When we read it, we reinforce assumptions and stories about Africa that we've heard throughout our lives. We reconfirm our image of Africa' (para. 1). 'So what is the answer? Western governments would like to be seen as generous beneficiaries, doing what they can to "help those unable to help themselves". But the first task is to stop perpetuating the harm they are doing' (*Ibid.*, para. 12).

Similarly, Aronson argues that misleading and biased narratives that depict and describe Africa and other developing countries in this way allow for a White supremacist project of domination (Aronson 2017). This narrative is logically framed so that any opposition to a White Savior coming to save the day is seen in a negative light. However, Cole avers, 'the White Savior supports brutal policies in the morning, founds charities in the afternoon, and receives awards in the evening' (*Ibid.*, p. 37). Some of the brutal policies have, in many ways, brutalized land rights. This paradox of brutal policies on the one hand and charities on the other is the topic of this chapter. This is an argument that was earlier buttressed by Rodney in that a critical element of modern development is that it expresses a certain exploitative relationship, to wit, the exploitation of a state by another state. All the so-called 'weak' economies in the world are being exploited by other economies, and the backwardness that the world is currently dealing with is a product of capitalist, colonial and neo-colonial exploitation (Rodney 1982).

In Uganda, many projects have been implemented by White 'saviors' to enhance land governance. For example, there was a World Bank Project on Land Administration Reforms aimed at 'increased ownership of land tenure by digitizing ownership records, such as title deeds and leases' (World Bank 2018). Indeed, this World Bank project, like many other donor-funded projects, is increasing 'local' and 'foreign' investor confidence. Yet, the same projects rarely answer the latent and sometimes manifest negative effects of such projects. When such effects become severe, the same donors come back as 'White Saviors' to address the same problems that they directly or indirectly created through the private corporate sector. Sometimes, there are White Saviors' institutions that fund the corporate sector, whose actions to secure land for investment have been violent–through land grabbing and violent land evictions–hence violating land rights, the most affected being the smallholder and subsistence farmers.

Therefore, White Saviorism continues to nurture and foster relationships that undesirably undermine the realization of land rights in Uganda. Whereas White Saviorism is construed as a generous undertaking, it masks exploitative frameworks and tendencies. The White Saviorism architecture continues to provide a perfect infrastructure for land rights violations in Uganda. It is evident that White Saviorism maintains weak policies plus legal, institutional and administrative regimes that enable the exploitation of land resources by the same 'White Saviors', aiding and undermining the realization of land rights of many Ugandans. Understanding White Saviorism underlines the perpetuation of gross injustice against Ugandans in many districts regarding access to and utilization of land. The current White Saviorism cannot claim to promote land-related freedom and justice immanent in international human rights instruments. At the same time, it is silent on the exploitation of land and other resources.

LAND GRABBING IN UGANDA

According to the National Household Survey Report 2019/20, Uganda has a total population of 41 million people and total area coverage of 199,807.4 km² (Uganda Bureau of Statistics 2011). Land is thus critical to many Ugandans, especially given that 85 percent of the rural population depends on it for livelihood and income (Owaraga 2012). Yet, Uganda has been the target of land grabbing, largely because is keen to attract foreign investment. This has caused problems for people who have traditional rights to the land. Reports of land seizures have been recorded in all parts of the country, with investment groups, companies, political groups and the government taking over land from local people. However, it is difficult to know exactly how much land is involved, but it is estimated that between 4 and 8 percent of land in Uganda is subject to foreign land 'transactions' (GRAIN 2011). Foreign companies or investors, with the help of national elites and governments, are the main negotiators and actors in the current wave of large-scale land purchases. Foreign private investors are supported by financial institutions, large agricultural companies and institutional investors (Cotula *et al.*, 2009).

According to FoodFirst Information and Action Network (2010), land grabbing is the acquisition and control of land on a large scale, either legally or illegally, for commercial / industrial production, which is disproportionate in size compared to the average landholding in the region. The Tirana Declaration defines land grabbing as any land deal that violates human rights. Such a deal does not rely on the free, prior and informed consent of affected land users. It does not rely on a comprehensive assessment or ignore social, economic and environmental impacts (including gender discrimination). It is not based on a transparent contract that sets clear and binding commitments on activities, employment and benefit-sharing, and it is not based on effective democratic planning, independent oversight and meaningful participation (International Land Coalition 2011).

LEGAL AND POLICY FRAMEWORK

According to the United Nations Office of the High Commissioner for Human Rights, 'Land is not a mere commodity, but an essential element for the realization of many human rights. For many people, land is a source of livelihood and is central to economic rights. Land is also often linked to peoples' identities and so is tied to social and cultural rights. The government of Uganda is a signatory to international, national, legal and policy regimes for land rights. Many international treaties, conventions and declarations protect land rights. Key among them are the Universal Declaration of Human Rights (Article 17), the International Covenant on Economic, Social and Cultural Rights (ICESCR) (Article 25) and the African Charter on Human and Peoples' Rights (Article 14). Article 25 of the ICESCR (1966) states that 'Nothing in the present Covenant shall be interpreted as impairing the inherent right of all peoples to enjoy and utilize fully and freely their natural wealth and resources'.

Therefore, under international human rights law, the Ugandan government, like other governments, has a duty to protect all citizens from all forms of human rights violations and abuses. In practice, the duty of protection imposes on the Ugandan government 'to effectively enforce the legal framework once it comes into force, to prevent abuses and to ensure accountability and reparation when abuses occur' (United Nations Office of the High Commissioner for Human Rights 2011). States are obliged to create an

148

environment conducive to human rights (Maastricht Principle 29, United Nations Convention Article 56 and Universal Declaration of Human Rights Article 28) in sensitive land contexts.

At the national level, Uganda has established a national law and policy that protects the right to access land. The Uganda Land Policy recognizes the problem of land grabbing in areas that are rich in resources, stating, 'cases of grabbing of land from Indigenous communities are common, as customary owners are insecure because they do not possess formalized rights over land to benefit from sharing of royalties as provided under the constitution'. However, the law is feeble, and in practice, the law disregards customary owners who find it hard to prove ownership when confronted with Western-backed companies.

PARADOX OF WHITE SAVIORISM AND LAND GRABBING

Land with natural resources and demarcated infrastructure projects is the main focus for land speculators in terms of land grabs and forced, as well as illegal, evictions. Compulsory land acquisitions continue to be illusionary among the various stakeholders operating in the affected communities and regions (Uganda Consortium on Corporate Accountability 2018). A few critical cases where the White Saviors support the corporate sector for investment but end up violating land rights are presented below.

Mubende District Case–Central Uganda

In August 2001, residents of the villages of Kiriyamakobe, Luwunga, Kitemba and Kijunga (about 24,000 people) in Uganda's Mubende District were pugnaciously evicted from the 2,524 hectares of land on which they had been living for years. With the support of local authorities, the Ugandan Army used violence against the community. The eviction came after Germany-based Neumann Kaffee Gruppe entered into a lease agreement with the Ugandan government to lease land for a coffee plantation (Muhindo 2017). After the eviction and without compensation to the evacuees, the land was leased to Kaweri Coffee Plantation Ltd., which is a 100 percent subsidiary of the Neumann Kaffee Gruppe. The coffee plantation was established on cleared land with the support of the German Development Agency and the African Development Bank (2010). During the evacuation, arson, brutality and grievous bodily harm were inflicted on residents. Houses were burned and destroyed, a fully equipped clinic and six churches, the movable property was looted, and crops were cut down and uprooted (*Ibid.*).

Conventionally, the German Development Agency is the development arm of the Government of Germany. Therefore, from the Mubende district case, it is apparent that the corporate sector, particularly Neumann Kaffee Gruppe represents the concealed exploitive interests coupled with a White Savior attitude by the German Government. In Uganda and possibly other African countries, there are many cases where the interests of the White Saviors are concealed and surreptitiously executed through the corporate sector. Such underhanded methods undermine human rights, including land rights, as evidenced in the Mubende district case.

Kiboga District Case–Central Uganda

In a report dated 22 September 2011, Oxfam reported to the European Investment Bank that, to allow New Forests Company Uganda U.K. Ltd., a subsidiary of New Forests Company in the United Kingdom, to plant and harvest timber in Uganda, more than 20,000 people were evicted between 2006 and 2010. The report further states that 'the people evicted from the land are desperate, having been driven into poverty and landlessness. In some instances, they were subjected to violence and their property, crops, and livestock were destroyed. They were not offered adequate compensation' (European Investment Bank 2014, p. 4). The project concerns the financing of the costs of Namwasa, the plantation of New Forests Company located in the Namwasa Central Forest reserve (8,000 ha), 120 km northwest of Kampala in the Mubende district. The project, which consists of planting fast-growing trees on degraded forest land, forms part of a larger New Forests program of three plantations covering a total of about 20,000 ha. The other plantations are the Luwanga Forest reserve (9,000 ha) in the Kiboga districts. In both Namwasa and Luwanga, the New Forests has a license agreement with the Uganda National Forest Authority. The Project Promoter, as well as Borrower of the direct loan of the European Investment Bank, is New Forests Company ($6.2 million). In comparison, indirect participation was made in AGRI-Vie FundPCC ($2 million), which holds an equity stake in New Forests. The conclusion of the investigation report states, 'Given the signature of the mediation agreements by the communities concerned, the European Investment Bank Complaint Mechanism considers that there is no need to proceed with the own full investigation and proceeds to close the case with the agreement of the President' (*Ibid.*, p. 6). In this chapter, I could not establish whether there was equity in the agreement between the community and new forests. Yet, the European Investment Bank could not go ahead and investigate this given that it had a conflict of interest–the Project Financier.

Similar to the Mubende case, the European Investment Bank and New Forests Company Uganda U.K. Ltd., a subsidiary of the New Forests Company (a United Kingdom-based corporation) represent the interest of Western agents with good intentions but exploitative practices, albeit obscured and disguised. For example, the website of the European Investment Bank states that they are 'the lending arm of the European Union. We are the biggest multilateral financial institution in the world' (European Investment Bank 2022). However, the bank further states that 'respect for human rights is a fundamental value at the European Investment Bank. Equality and human dignity are central to our mission' (European Investment Bank 2022). In practice, the funding from the European Investment Bank continues to undermine land rights and other related human rights of Ugandans.

The Kalangala District Case–Central Uganda

The Government of Uganda, the World Bank, the International Fund for Agricultural Development and Wilmar International, one of the world's largest oilseed companies in the world, launched the Vegetable Oil Development Project in 1998. The project, in partnership with the Kenya Oilseed Company BIDCO, is developing palm oil plantations in the Kalangala district of Uganda, on the shores of Lake Victoria. The first phase of the project was completed in 2011, and although some social and environmental problems have arisen, the second phase of the project is ongoing. The second phase of palm oil plantations even expanded to several other islands. The project is promoted as an effort to reduce poverty, but it causes displacement, food insecurity and deforestation. There are serious questions about donor financing and the rationale for private investment in the project.

With the above cases, the European Investment Bank, the World Bank and other multilateral financial institutions and multilateral corporations exist to advance the agenda of capital accumulation. In the process of advancing this agenda, the corporate sector inevitably creates interlinked problems, such as the violation of land rights that necessitate the intervention of the White Saviors, hence a never-ending cycle of their relevance.

In addition, from the above cases, the corporate sector becomes agents of the White Saviors, who facilitate capital and profit accumulation, which is later used by the White Saviors to dominate the 'poor countries'. In the process of profit accumulation, they cause a lot of challenges, such as the dispossession of land, a critical factor in the livelihood of subsistence farmers who are forced into poverty. White Saviors see many Ugandans as poor and in need of help and are busy designing programs for poverty reduction, while the corporate sector is actively exploiting Uganda's land and other natural resources, which enhances their home economies. This exploitation by the corporate sector inevitably precipitates many development challenges, such as land and property dispossession, causing increasing poverty among the local farmers who depend on that land for a livelihood, hence creating an unending cycle.

Therefore, as Uganda receives a lot of aid, which is part of the White Saviorism industrial complex, the reality is that many countries that offer aid with their right hand take a lot more with their left hand (through corporations). In this case, it is indistinct whether such countries are saviors or not. What we call 'aid' for countries such as Uganda is not aid, given that these countries have given more than what they receive through colonialism, slavery and actual unfair trade agreements. To foreign corporations and governments, accessing land in Uganda is akin to a self-service buffet. In fact, many Ugandans need more reparation for the harm being done to them, not monies handed out as charity and certainly not as a means by other countries to further their own interests (Kagal 2021).

Corporations also collude with some government officials. Through this collusion, the Government of Uganda 'plays a triple role as; sellers, acquirers, and facilitators of the process of Large Scale Land Acquisitions or land grabbing' (Fonjong 2017, p. 47). The government thus plays a key role in favouring companies that take over community land with or without due process (*Ibid.*). Simultaneously, the government then accepts the help given by the host countries of these companies.

GRABBING LAND TO ENTRENCH SUPREMACY

Cases such as the Mubende, Kalangala and Kiboga captured above demonstrate that Uganda, like other African countries, receives less from its resources compared to the aid that the government receives. Analogously, Dearden (2017) finds that Sub-Saharan Africa is a net creditor to the rest of the world with over $41 billion. Whereas there is money coming in, about $161 billion per year, there is $203 billion that leaves the continent in loans, remittances (workers outside Africa) and benefits. Some of that money, about $68 billion, goes out in the form of evaded taxes. International corporations cheat and steal much of it–lawfully–by pretending to actually make wealth in tax sanctuaries and havens. In addition, 'there's the $30 billion these companies "return"–profits they made in Africa but sent back home or elsewhere to enjoy their wealth' (*Ibid.*, para. 4). In any case, Dearden's assessment is very generous because it assumes that all the aid flowing into Africa benefits the people of that continent, a fallacious and skewed argument.

Poor smallholder farmers–the backbone of agriculture and food security–can hardly compete favourably with large-scale agro-investors. In most cases, smallholder farmers have been 'swallowed' by large-scale investors masking the creation of jobs while at the same time exploiting the local workers that provide cheap labour (Mabikke 2011). Many of the rural farmers who give up their farmlands to get 'better jobs' become modern slaves to manipulative and exploitative investors (*Ibid.*). The White Saviors are requested to come in urgently and address the problem of increasing poverty largely occasioned by the corporate sector.

Carmody and Taylor (2016) contend that the major land grabs in Uganda and Africa in general 'are a product of ecological scarcity and the opportunities this presents for accumulation and logics of state-building. In effect, land grabs represent a re-inscription and deepening of socio-spatial power inequalities associated with previous eras' (Carmody and Taylor 2016, p. 100). However, I argue that major land grabs in Uganda, particularly in Kalangala, Kiboga and Mubende, were driven by the insatiable greed for wealth accumulation of affluent corporations and states and their hidden need to entrench supremacy. This hegemony masks exploitation, with attendant development challenges to be later addressed by the White Saviors.

The state, companies and investors that give and acquire lease or sell land, respectively, argue that most of the land that is given out is either 'unproductive' or 'underutilized'. I argue that this existential dominance underlines White supremacy and economic egotism–thinking that state and foreign corporations' activities are more important than the communities' activities. This is because the construct of underutilization denotes unequal power relations in the decision of whether to take over the land or not by the corporate sector supported by the state machinery. It should be underlined, 'there are types of land use such as; grazing animals, collecting firewood and medicinal plants for the poor.

These uses are rarely included in the official appraisal of projects as they are not marketed, yet they are vital sources of livelihoods for the poor' (Braun and Meinzen-Dick 2009).

Uganda is hitherto unequipped to deal with large-scale land tenure and land grab challenges. The government should develop robust frameworks to protect the rights of local communities, the poor and the vulnerable (Dearden 2017).

Large-scale land seizures also have serious consequences for the civil and political rights of the affected people. As Cotula (2014) pointed out, 'At root, "land grabbing" is an issue of democratic governance—who makes decisions, whose voices are heard, and what space is available for dissent' (Cotula 2014, p. 21). In the above cases, decisions were made by corporations, supported by the state apparatus, with no or limited room for dissent. Businesses and private investors often claim that consultations have taken place and local communities agree. Often, however, there is insufficient evidence to confirm that affected people have participated, accepted, consented or refused the start-up of such projects.

In cases where land rights are violated, such as the Mubende case, communities face great obstacles in obtaining adequate and fair compensation. The harm and human rights impact caused by the projects in question continue to adversely and painfully affect people even when such projects end. Above all, projects often do not foresee land justice and other human rights redress beyond the project lifespan. It is important to conduct human rights analysis on all aspects of planned development projects to predict and mitigate aggravating human rights violations and to prohibit the physical removal of people from their land without their informed consent.

CONCLUSION

This chapter examines the White Saviorism, the corporate sector and land rights violation nexus in Uganda. Vividly, the wanton yet exploitative acquisition of large-scale land and the attendant violation of land rights by the corporate sector in Uganda is primarily propelled by profit (Fonjong 2017). Yet, the kleptocrats and rackets of unregulated foreign corporations are behind large-scale land acquisitions and violations of the land rights of local smallholder farmers. Some of the White Saviors hide behind the corporate sector, which continues exploiting land resources in Uganda, which later leads to the violation of land rights.

The only variance between wholesale land and other natural resource expropriation during colonial times and the post-independence era is only the new players and beneficiaries. Instead of contributing to development—as always advanced by the government of Uganda—large-scale land purchases by the corporate sector—hailing from White Savior countries—often negatively integrate individuals and communities into global value chains. In most cases, they result in a dependency on such companies and a complete loss of independence and violations of land rights and other rights.

The development challenges that are created by the corporate sector, such as the increasing levels of vulnerability and powerlessness among the project-affected persons, create an impetus for White Saviors to intervene and improve the situation. This White Savior intervention can be direct or indirect—through local civil society organizations. Yet, the role of the corporate sector in creating these conditions continues to be ignored, to the extent of not being mentioned by the White Saviors during their interventions and discussions. It appears that this lack of mention is deliberate so that the

White Saviors continue nurturing and sustaining their relevance in solving development problems caused by the corporate sector. This would imply that the corporate sector continues to 'create jobs for them'–by creating or causing more development challenges. In the words of Sandra Bullock at the Oscars, 'there is no race, no religion, no class system, no colour, nothing, no sexual orientation, that makes us better than anyone else. We are all deserving of love' (Moms, 2010). Therefore, all human beings, including Ugandans, deserve genuine love and genuine development partners without a hidden agenda.

REFERENCES

Anderson, A. (2013) 'Teach for America and the dangers of deficit thinking', *Critical Education*, vol. 4, no. 11:2-47

Aronson, B.A. (2017) 'The White Savior industrial complex: A cultural studies analysis of a teacher educator, savior film, and future teachers', *Journal of Critical Thought and Praxis*, vol. 6, no. 3:36-54

Carmody, P. and Taylor, D. (2016) 'Globalization, land grabbing, and the present-day colonial state in Uganda: Ecolonization and its impacts', *Journal of Environment and Development*, vol. 25, no. 1:100-126

Cotula, L. (2014) *Addressing the Human Rights Impacts of 'Land Grabbing', Study for the European Parliament*, Brussels, Think Tank European Parliament, European Union

Cotula, L., Vermeulen, S., Leonard, R. and Keeley, J. (2009) *Land Grab or Development Opportunity? Agricultural Investment and International Land Deals in Africa*, London/Rome, IIED, FAO and IFAD

Dearden, N. (2017) 'Africa is not poor, we are stealing its wealth, It's time to change the way we talk and think about Africa', *Aljazeera*, 24 May, https://www.aljazeera.com/opinions/2017/5/24/africa-is-not-poor-we-are-stealing-its-wealth, accessed 5 December 2022

European Investment Bank (2014) 'Conclusions Report', *NFC Forestry Project*, Complaint MCIE12011/13

European Investment Bank (2022) 'Who we are', EIB, https://www.eib.org/en/about/cr/human-rights/index.htm, accessed 25 March 2022

Fonjong, L. (2017) *Interrogating Large-Scale Land Acquisition and Its Implications for Women's Land Rights in Cameroon, Ghana and Uganda*, Ottawa, Canada, International DevelopmentResearch Centre

FoodFirst Information and Action Network (2010) *Annual Report 2010*, Heidelberg, Germany, FAIN International

GRAIN (2011) 'Extent of farmland grabbing for food production by foreign interests', https://grain.org/article/entries/4479-grain-releases-data-set-with-over-400-global-land-grabs, accessed 12 November 2022

International Land Coalition (2011) *Tirana Declaration*

Kagal, N. (2021) 'We need to talk: Reckonings in the international development sector, can development aid ever be anti-racist?', *The Medium*, 21 February

Mabikke, S.B. (2011) 'Large-scale land acquisitions for investment in Uganda: Can it yield equitable benefits for smallholder farmers?', paper presented at the *Trapca Sixth Annual Conference*, Arusha, Tanzania, 24-25 November

Moms (2010) 'Sandra Bullock recognizes all mothers in Oscar acceptance', *Pop Sugar*, 7 March

Muhindo, J. (2017) 'Compulsory Land Acquisition in Uganda an Analysis of the Proposed Amendment of Article 26 of the Constitution', Advocates Coalition for Development and Environment, ACODE Policy Briefing Paper Series No. 47, 2017

Owaraga, N. (2012) 'Conflict in Uganda's land tenure system', *Africa Portal, Backgrounder*, Johannesburg, https://www.africaportal.org/publications/conflict-in-ugadans-land-tenure/, accessed 20 January 2022

Rodney, W. (1982) *How Europe Under Developed Africa*, Washington, DC, Howard University Press

Sturges, K.M. (2015) *NeoLiberalizing Educational Reform, America's Quest for Profitable Market-Colonies and the Undoing of Public*

Good, Bold Visions in Educational Research, https://www.scribd.com/document/354273366/Keith-M-Sturges-Eds-Neoliberalizing-Educational-Reform-America-s-Quest-for-Profitable-Market-Colonies-and-the-Undoing-of-Public-Good, accessed 17 December 2021

The Monitor (2017) 'Gold miners on Buhweju district are facing eviction', *The Monitor*, 9 July, https://voice.global/assets/2019/03/The-women-who-toil-in-Buhwejus-gold-pits.pd, accessed 19 February 2022

Uganda Consortium on Corporate Accountability (2018) *Handbook on Land Ownership, Rights, Interests and Acquisition in Uganda*, UCCA, https://ucca-uganda.org/wp-content/uploads/2020/03/Handbook-on-Land-Rights-Interests-and-Acquisition-Processes-in-Uganda.pdf, accessed 15 November 2021

United Nations Office of the High Commissioner for Human Rights (2011) 'Guiding principles on business and human rights: Implementing the United Nations 'Protect, Respect, and Remedy Framework', New York, United Nations, https://www.ohchr.org/sites/default/files/documents/publications/guidingprinciplesbusinesshr_en.pdf, accessed 15 July 2021

United Nations Office of the High Commissioner for Human Rights (1966) 'International covenant on economic, social and cultural rights', New York, United Nations, https://www.ohchr.org/en/instruments-mechanisms/instruments/international-covenant-economic-social-and-cultural-rights, accessed 17 October 2021

World Bank (2018) *Land Administration Reforms Cut the Red Tape*, Washington, DC, World Bank, 20 April, https://www.worldbank.org/en/news/feature/2018/04/20/land-administration-reforms-cut-the-red-tape, accessed 17 October 2021

PART II

LIVED EXPERIENCES

9

White Saviorism, Green Colonialism and Sea Shepherd

Fernando David Márquez Duarte

F
isheries of coastal towns in México, such as San Felipe and the Cucapáh, where Indigenous people live and fish in the Colorado River delta, have suffered from conflicts due to the existence of endangered species of fish in the Gulf of California, especially the totoaba and the vaquita marina. The presence of these endangered species has led the federal government to decree a permanent closed season for them that has been going on for decades. However, the banning of fishing these species in the Colorado River delta and the port of San Felipe has caused poverty and violence against the fishers in the zone. The complete prohibition of its fishing for several years has affected local fishers who practice survival fishing for other species that are not endangered. This issue has been exacerbated in the last few years due to the actions of the Western Non-Governmental Organization (NGO) Sea Shepherd, which has attacked the local fishers with their vessels, reaching the point of killing a fisherman in San Felipe in January 2021. I analyze how Sea Shepherd and other Western organizations inflict neo-colonial practices against the local fishers under the practice of green colonialism in alliance

with México's government, manifesting a clear attitude of White Saviorism.

In recent years, the Colorado River delta and the small port of San Felipe, both in the municipality of Mexicali, Baja California (México), have suffered poverty and violence due to federal restrictions on fishing and, more recently, due to the intervention of Western NGOs that seek to 'protect' the fish. However, they have caused more damage than good. The most (in)famous of these NGOs is Sea Shepherd, which was founded in California, United States of America (USA), but has had to move to other venues due to the legal processes that it has faced for violent and illegal actions.

VIOLENCE AND SUBJUGATION OF FISHERS
IN THE GULF OF CALIFORNIA

The conflict centers upon the following situation: the *totoaba* and *vaquita marina* are banned to fish; however, in the zones where these fish are known to live, other species are allowed to be fished, such as the *curvina golfina*, that fishers of the zone rely on, to sell and survive. This has led to the criminalization of the fishers, both part of the Cucapáh (a word that means people of the river in their language) Indigenous group and non-Indigenous fishers. If any fisher is seen in the zones of the *totoaba* and *vaquita marina*, they are targeted not only by the military but, more dangerously, by Sea Shepherd. The military can stop the fishers and see if they are fishing any banned species, but Sea Shepherd's ship does not care to see if they are fishing any endangered species. They attack the fishers' *pangas* (small boats that small fishers have traditionally used for decades) by ramming them with their ship and attacking them with water cannons similar to those used by military forces. These attacks by Sea Shepherd's

Farley Mowat ship have caused serious injuries to several fishers in the port of San Felipe and the death of at least two fishers (Heras 2021).

To dive deeper into the situation, it is necessary to track Sea Shepherd's history and the conflicts that it has caused in different countries. Sea Shepherd was founded in 1977 by Paul Watson, who was kicked out of Greenpeace that same year due to his violent actions, such as armed assaults against fishers (Influence Watch 2021). Sea Shepherd is a *vigilante* group that preaches to protect and defend endangered maritime species. However, they do this by attacking fishing boats and destroying them with violent tactics (as the ones mentioned before), causing injuries and deaths of several fishers around the world. The organization has, as a result, been expelled and prohibited in five countries, including the state of California. In Japan, they are considered a terrorist group (Domínguez 2021). Moreover, an individual who witnessed first-hand the actions and tactics of the *Farley Mowat* in San Felipe declared that several of the crew members have been in jail or have legal processes against them for aggression and violence in different countries and that they do not care about the lives and survival of the fishers in the zone. Watson himself has been in jail in Canada and the Netherlands, as well as investigated in Costa Rica for attempting to murder local fishers.

It is worth considering that this NGO has millions of dollars in income due to large donations from wealthy artists such as Leonardo Di Caprio, Mick Jagger, Sean Penn, Uma Thurman, Pierce Brosnan, Edward Norton, just to mention a few. Under the guise of 'saving' the fish, Sea Shepherd earns millions of dollars and continues to attack local fishers in the Gulf of California with impunity. As of today, the organization and / or the crew of the *Farley Mowat* have not faced any legal charges, and curiously, the ship disappeared from the zone, and its current location is unknown.

The lack of attention to the violent practices of this NGO is not a coincidence, considering that it is owned and composed mostly of White Westerners and is financed and publicly supported by wealthy White artists. I contend that this is a clear indicator of White Saviorism, granting this organization an 'untouchable' status, getting away with murder, assault and other violent crimes against people in San Felipe and masking their utter disdain for the life and health of Mexican people under an argument of 'saving the fish'.

This is where green colonialism directly manifests. This term can be understood as a neo-colonial process where environmental protection speeches are used by Western business and political elites (allied with elites in 'developing' countries) to justify and further perpetuate processes of dispossession and subjugation of marginalized groups (Normann 2021).

THE CUCAPÁH PEOPLES

Moreover, the situation of fishing in the area has negatively affected people of the Cucapáh Indigenous group, most of whom live in the Indigenous community of *El Mayor Cucapáh*, on the outskirts of the municipality of Mexicali. The Cucapáh people have fished for centuries in the area, which has been and still is their main economic activity. However, the banning of fishing by the federal government has not only been on San Felipe's coast but also in the Gulf of California, including the Colorado River *delta*, which is where the Cucapáh has always fished. The zone of the Delta was established by the federal government as a natural reserve, prohibiting fishing in the area for commercial purposes. However, the Cucapáh fishers are only a few dozen that fish small amounts of curvina to survive.

Some of the Cucapáh fishers got special permits to fish; however, non-Indigenous people have taken advantage of these permits and have used them illegally, making the government put the blame on the Cucapáh people and limiting the amount of fishing allowed. Added to this situation, the Cucapáh have been affected for decades by the deviation of the Colorado River water by the United States into their cities, especially with the dozens of dams created to limit the flow of water that gets into México. This situation has dried up the arm of Colorado that is in the Cucapáh community known as *Hardy River*.

The drying of the Hardy, as well as the banning of the fishing species, has caused not only poverty but also the death of a part of the Cucapáh culture since their cosmovision depends on the river. The Cucapáh people complain that projects that directly affect them and their ancestral lands, such as the binational water treaty between the United States and México and projects to restore the *humedales* of the river, have never been consulted with them.

Even if international treaties like Convention 169 of the International Labour Organization (ILO) (1989) or the Declaration of the United Nations on the Rights of Indigenous Peoples (United Nations 2007) have specific articles that establish free and informed consultation with Indigenous people as their right about projects and policies that affect them and their ancestral territory. They have also complained that for projects such as the establishment of the transnational brewery constellation brands in Mexicali, they were not consulted. That project would have taken an extreme amount of water that would have left them with less water in their community. The brewery began to build a plant to produce beer and sell it outside of México, which would take an enormous amount of water, depleting the reserves of the city and of the region. This project was established without the government consulting the population, and there were massive protests against it from 2017 to 2020, leading to the official cancellation of the project in 2020 (Duarte 2020).

CONCLUSION

The struggle to survive and protect the right to fish is a very difficult situation that sadly affects both the Cucapáh Indigenous people and the fishers of San Felipe. In these cases, Western NGOs, such as Sea Shepherd, clearly shows White Saviorism, where they preach an image of saviors of fish, but at the expense of causing conflicts, injuries and even deaths of Mexican fishers. This perpetuates neo-colonialism under a progressive mask, with the same essence and logic of neo-colonialism: the thought that their cause is the only valuable thing and that their lives are more valuable than the lives and wellbeing of people in the Global South, oppressing the fishers of the zone with coloniality of power.

REFERENCES

Domínguez, A. (2021) 'Quieren Pescadores Salida de Sea Sheperd', La Voz de La Frontera, 3 January, https://www.lavozdelafrontera.com.mx/local/sea-sheperd-criminaliza-la-pesca-de-san-felipe-alejandra-leon-6244140.html, accessed 5 December 2022

Duarte, F.D.M. (2020) 'Las resistencias organizadas por la defensa del agua vs Coparmex y Constellation Brands', 15diario.com, 28 March, https://15diario.com/las-resistencias-organizadas-por-la-defensa-del-agua-vs-coparmex-y-constellation-brands-fernando-david-marquez-duarte.html, accessed 5 December 2022

Heras, A. (2021) 'Acusan a Sea Shepherd de asesinar a un pescador de San Felipe', La Jornada, 5 January, https://

www.jornada.com.mx/notas/2021/01/05/estados/acusan-a-sea-shepherd-de-asesinar-a-un-pescador-de-san-felipe/, accessed 5 December 2022

Influence Watch (2021) 'Sea Shepherd Conservation Society', https://www.influencewatch.org/non-profit/sea-shepherd-conservation-society/, accessed 6 March 2022

Normann, S. (2021) 'Green colonialism in the Nordic context: Exploring Southern Saami representations of wind energy development', *Journal of Community Psychology*, vol. 49, no. 1:77-94

Organización Internacional del Trabajo (1989) 'Convenio Número 169 de la OIT sobre Pueblos Indígenas y Tribales', https://www.ilo.org/wcmsp5/groups/public/---americas/---ro-lima/documents/publication/wcms_345065.pdf, accessed 28 March 2022

10

Today as Yesterday, the 'Savior Complex' of Europeans

Anonymous 1[1]

In the 21st century, the practice of ethnotourism or ecotourism is on the rise. It is a practice described as tourism 'where the other, the native, represents a way of life opposed to modernity', and because of this, tourists 'have a curious eye for the other, that is different,' in a 'face-to-face between two extreme otherness: the modern and cultivated tourists, and the natives who represent the non-modern world' (Hernández 2015). Curiosity, therefore, pushes the ethnos and ecotourists to go discover these people who have not bitten into modernity. However, this practice is not free from the trap of White Saviorism.

A White Saviorism that blinds some tourists despite their desire to be 'correct' and 'ethical' is sometimes blatant. I was 10 years old when some tourists passing through my village of Kabare in South Kivu (Democratic Republic of the Congo) gave us a package, an improvised gift in thanks for the spontaneous welcome we had given them. They said that they didn't have much left to give us to thank us, as if they had to give something. After they left, the person who opened the bag

---

[1] Translated from French

found some badly wrapped candy, some medicine that was about to expire and some underwear that was probably destined for the garbage. In short, nothing of value. The adults burned everything to prevent the children from consuming it, especially the unclean candy. If it weren't for White Saviorism that considers Africans to be on the receiving end of everything, these tourists would never have dared to give such a package. But let's talk about White Saviorism in international tourism with some recent facts.

In April 2021, a group of European tourists arrived in a village in Central Africa to discover the Aka people, a community mistakenly called 'Pygmies', meaning 'as big as a fist'. Moreover, the visit occurred in the middle of the global COVID-19 pandemic. A person who is very close to me shared her concerns about tourists in the territory where she works. Shortly thereafter, this group posted a video on YouTube. She sent me the link to see what had happened, and I found that she had reason to be concerned. Unfortunately, tourists do not always go to Africa, considering themselves equal to African people, and this has an impact on the people they meet.

If the tourists decided to visit that community in Africa and if they have had some preparation for this trip and the way of life of these people to meet, they still, obviously, did not receive training on the possible consequences of their actions and words throughout their visit. Moreover, the visited ones still needed to decide to welcome the tourists, and worse, they needed to prepare for this visit. Indeed, there was neither their prior consent nor knowledge of the tourists' way of life. As soon as the tourists arrived in the village, the people were seized by terror. One girl even trembled with all her being. The tourists used the backs and heads of the villagers to put their luggage for a four-day portage service, leaving them with back wounds at the end of the trip. They all received the equivalent of €20, more than enough for the tourists. During their visit, the tourists learned different knowledge from the Aka people, especially how to quench their thirst without water by using a forest branch, how to heal wounds quickly and how to walk in the forest while protecting themselves from ant hills. The tourists offered modern gifts to their hosts, including a few packets of sugar, matches, soap and arrows for hunting. They also received chickens as gifts. When the time came to give these gifts to the Aka people, individuals from the neighbouring village were present and wanted to have some too. The tourists then brought them back to order, explaining that the gifts were intended for the Aka people, who were always victims of the Bantu people, who, themselves, could easily obtain such things.

Trivial facts, many would say. However, important things are at stake here.

First, the Aka men and women have been living in the forest for thousands of years, feeding on the fruits of the forest. By offering arrows and matches to them, it implies that their knowledge of fire and hunting arrows production will be forgotten as they will turn to the acquisition of matches and arrows made in Europe. However, if the first samples are given to them as gifts, the next ones will have to be paid for at a high financial cost. Their descendants, who will no longer have learned to produce their arrows and their own fire, will have to depend on the West for delivery. This way, under the guise of help, the tourists actually destroyed the Aka people's ways of living. This is what the White Saviorism produces.

Then, it should be pointed out here that the tourists arrived in the middle of the COVID-19 pandemic. It is not excluded that this virus will enter this yet unreached forest. Moreover, they offered packets of refined sugar, even though no one knew the devastating effects of sugar on human health. The illnesses that the Aka people will develop due to this consumption are not included in their repertoire of illnesses and remedies to treat. They will once again have to turn to Europe for treatment.

On the other hand, the tourists have learned how to take care of their wounds. This course is free, total and brief, as, in the space of a few minutes, the knowledge is transmitted and learned. In a way, it is the Aka people's way of helping Europeans to learn other forms of knowledge. However, if in a few years, a young Aka decides to go and learn how these visitors heal their wounds, s/he will have to invest several years in school to learn the language, go through long procedures to get a visa and pay a great deal of money for his rent and his courses. S/he will have to pay for the equivalent of what his parents or grandparents received for free.

But that's not all. We must also take a look at the reproduction of a colonial past in this visit.

COLONIZATION, TODAY AS YESTERDAY

At the base of the colonization of Africa, writers speak of the five Cs (Surun 2006), namely 'curiosity, civilization, Christianity, commerce and colonization'. The first C, which is curiosity, carried by the explorers, had opened the door to the other Cs of which the fifth, colonization, still weighs today in the life of African men and women because of the many traumas that it generated. This famous curiosity provided useful information for the interests of the West, facilitating the division and sharing of Africa as well as the total submission of the peoples whose culture and customs they had already mastered. Years later, the colonizers used this knowledge to better destroy the culture of the colonized under the pretext of civilizing them.

On the other hand, humanitarian motives have served as a cover for establishing the colonial system. When King Leopold II wanted to take over the immense territory of the Congo, he justified his actions by claiming he wanted to save the people from slavery. However, as we know, he cut off the hands of the Congolese and imposed deadly work on them. This resulted in the first, yet unrecognized, Congolese genocide between 1885 and 1908 (Wiltz 2020). This logic of 'saving' the souls of colonized peoples led to cultural genocide. It is also known that Western merchants during the colonial era practiced bartering, raiding the wealth of Africa and giving junk in exchange. But let's get back to the most important point, that of division and the seed of conflict.

To subdue the African peoples during colonization, the 'divide and rule' approach was ingeniously applied. Some say that among the Rwandans, for example, this way of ruling worked perfectly. In Rwanda, the three groups, Hutu, Tutsi and Twa, lived peacefully together until one group was elevated above the others. The Tutsis were considered by the colonists to be the most intelligent, the biggest, the most honest and the richest, who had cows and land to distribute to the poor Hutus and Twas, farmers and hunter-gatherers, respectively. The latter, considered second and third-class citizens, were to be subjugated to the first-class Tutsi citizens.

Later, the same colonists, considering the abuse of power by the Tutsis unbearable, established the Hutus as a victimized majority, oppressed by the Tutsi minority and gave them power and solid support. In 1994, it was the turn of the Hutus to be designated as *genocidaires* and the Tutsis as victims. Thus, an endless cycle of victim–victimization was established in Rwanda.

The similarities are obvious with the Aka people. They were once referred to as 'pygmies'–the word itself speaks volumes–

173

compared to other villagers who were considered larger, richer, and more 'civilized'. And even today, unfortunately, the current tourists perpetuate these clichés. If the tourists have not realized it, it should be emphasized here that calling the Aka people 'pygmies', as opposed to other villagers of a different group whom they call 'Bantu', creates a categorization that immediately places the former as inferior, the latter as superior, while the ethnotourists drape themselves in a complex of saviors of the Aka people. But when there was genocide in Rwanda, for example, it was the Rwandans who exterminated each other while relying on the same saviors who sowed the seeds of the hegemony of one over the other.

In addition to triggering the hatred of one ethnic group against another, we can underline other forms of division of colonial origin. The hostility between religions is one of them. The same is true for African men who have internalized that they are superior to women. All these assertions of superiority of some over others, as well as the victimization of those who end up paying the price of these deadly divisions, are an emanation of colonization carried by Westerners draped in their White Saviorism Complex of coming to civilize Africans while dividing them. Everything depends on the interests of the moment in the West, to make some play the role of superiors, and others, the role of inferiors. In turn, each one passes from executioner to victim, and the cycle continues under the arbitration of the West.

However, something good came out of the ethnotourists' visit: the presentation of a documentary to the Aka people. The film was about the ancestral way of life of people living a way of life similar to the one lived by the Aka people. We see the know-how of the elders to build liana bridges. In a way, it shows the current generations part of what they have lost of their culture. In fact, the cultural genocide that struck all colonized peoples did not spare the Aka people either. But they have done their best to preserve as much of their way of life as possible, and that is why tourists are interested in them. During this visit, some tourists could have taken the time to value the way of life of the community they met, explain to them why they are interested in it, and better yet, show a documentary on the ancient life in Western countries' countryside. By creating a better human-to-human connection, it would have encouraged the Aka people to be proud of themselves while recognizing that Westerners who come to visit them are not superhuman.

Ethnotourism as practiced in Africa, needs to be reviewed and rethought. Tourists and their guides should learn about colonial times and their consequences if they want to avoid reproducing detrimental effects on the host communities. Suppose this type of tourism was practiced in a different way, with an attitude of mutual enrichment through the sharing of knowledge and mutual respect from human to human. In that case, the future could change and differ from former North-South relations. It is now, in the present, that we need to achieve the rupture with the characteristic paternalism of the White Saviorism of the West.

REFERENCES

Hernández, K.L. (2015) 'Une expérience de voyage éco et ethno-touristique chez les Wayuu. Témoignage et analyse', *Elohi*, 7:49-73

Surun, I. (2006) 'L'exploration de l'Afrique au XIXe siècle: une histoire précoloniale au regard des postcolonial studies', *Revue d'histoire du XIXe siècle*, 32:21-9

Wiltz, M. (2020) *Il pleut des mains sur le Congo*, Paris, Éditions Magellan & Cie

11

SUVs, Hotels and Faith:
Experiences of White Privilege

Amjad Mohamed Saleem

These experiences are based on my reflections when I was deployed on a post-tsunami and post-conflict support mission to Sri Lanka from 2005 to 2009. It was a baptism of fire around White Saviorism, racism, power and privilege, which taught me that international Non-Governmental Organizations (NGOs) and international humanitarian and development work have to change so that the national staff is treated the same as international staff. Communities should also be provided with an agency to be part of the conversation. And finally, working for a faith-based organization (FBO) should not be seen as negative. My experience in Sri Lanka made me realize that power and privilege were proportionally related to funding and that where you come from did not necessarily correspond to better treatment. In fact, often, it was your color, age and gender that mattered.

FOREIGN VERSUS 'LOCAL' EXPERIENCES

In 2005, four months after the devastating tsunami that hit Sri Lanka in December 2004, I was in the country of my heritage, working for a British-Muslim NGO sent out to build houses for tsunami-displaced people in the East. I am in a unique position: the 'foreigner' with a local touch. I was the guinea pig for the charity that had hitherto been working with local partners in Sri Lanka and had a 'local' presence, but due to the nature of the tsunami and the funding generated, had opted to have a presence in-country to oversee some of the delivery as per the requirement of the donor. I was the compromise candidate, someone who was 'local' in that I had Sri Lankan heritage and so could meet the charity's interest in going local and also someone who was British, so meeting the donor requirements. Somehow in those days, it was felt that someone external would be less prone to corruption than someone internal. Sadly, from many experiences we have heard over the last few years, this is not necessarily true, and internationals are just as corrupt as locals.

In 2005, the concept of localization was not high on the donors' agenda. Yet, here was a charity that was actually willing to invest in that perspective, a diaspora member who could relate to both sides of the spectrum. Yet to my surprise, I encountered a lot of skepticism and resistance from colleagues in the International NGO (INGO) and United Nations sectors who were suspicious as to whether I would be impartial and neutral or whether I could be swayed by political persuasion. There was no thought or consideration for my agency, and the default opinion was that somehow I was weak.

The reaction from my Sri Lankan colleagues was somewhat different. There was initially a belief that I did not have the correct skills or knowledge, and often I found that when I spoke, I was dismissed. If someone else said the same thing, especially someone who seemed to be a lot more senior or White, it was readily accepted. So from Sri Lankan colleagues, it became an issue of age, perceptions of inexperience and color. In those early days, I learned to choose my battles and to pick my allies and 'spokespeople', i.e., those people who would effectively communicate my ideas on my behalf. I thought of myself as the 'consigliere' or the advisor to others.

At first, I also glossed over my Sri Lankan heritage, and when people made the mistake of thinking I was Pakistani and not Sri Lankan because of my Muslim name, I did not really correct them. To this day, I am surprised at how ignorant people were of the history and composition of Sri Lanka. Many foreigners deployed there did not know there was a Muslim community that was present in Sri Lanka and also affected by the conflict. They saw Sri Lanka as a binary community between the Sinhalese and the Tamils without any appreciation for the rich religious and ethnic diversity it had. There was a basic unwillingness to learn about the country before coming out to work there. I also can't count the number of times my name had been mispronounced or basically not understood. I became AJ, Jad, Amstrad because it was 'difficult to learn my name'. Nevertheless, I was happy to play the foreigner because that allowed me to finish my work. Still, I did feel that tension of an identity crisis, trying to desperately fit in with the other 'expats' whilst staying true to my heritage. It was not until the second half of my second year that I got the confidence to get out of my shell to challenge those stereotypes and assert who I was. Yet those first 18 months were difficult, trying to understand where I fit in.

WHITE SUVS AND WHITE SAVIORISM

My first encounter with White Saviorism in international development and humanitarian action was sitting in a coordination meeting and being grilled about who my 'beneficiaries' were and being challenged as to whether I could live up to the Humanitarian Principles or not. The question started with 'Are you just working with Muslim beneficiaries?' and 'Are you Saudi-funded?' when I introduced myself, before being asked blatantly, 'Do you follow the Humanitarian Principles'. Being the apologetic Muslim after 9/11 who was going out of my way to let people know I was not a terrorist and that my organization did not support terror, I duly obliged. My lesson from that incident was to introduce myself as 'Hi, I'm Amjad, I am working for XXXX, a British Muslim NGO operating worldwide and funded by British Muslims. We are a signatory of the Red Cross Code of Conduct and follow the Humanitarian Principles'. This became my mantra because I had to allay people's fears that somehow we were not a terror-funding organization.

What bothered me was the expectation that I would have to explain myself when I introduced myself when I didn't see that expectation put on others, especially Christian NGOs. The irony of the situation of that first meeting, in hindsight, was the fact that there were representatives from two European Christian faith-based NGOs, who, like me, had just arrived and were introducing themselves and were not asked the same questions. To this day, I still see that just as there is a privilege in terms of country and color, there is a privilege in terms of faith. Some faith-based NGOs have to justify why they need a seat at the table, while others do not, especially if they have tacit government support.

Part of this reason for having to always explain myself was also related to the fact that I was not in the same social circles as the majority of 'expats' working in the NGO or diplomatic sector, who would meet at embassy parties or hang out at the swimming pools of 5-star hotels on the weekend. As a result, I missed out on the nuances of the friendship of being drinking buddies and dinner companions hanging out together in the evenings and weekends. I never realized this until certain meetings where people would reference a previous evening's party or a weekend trip to the beach. What I began to realize is that a social network is important for building relationships at work.

I realized that these social networks spilled over into the professional network where work and partnerships were shared between 'friends', and even though things were done on a professional basis, it was clear that personal friendships were important. You worked with people that you knew, and much of the time, you knew them because you had gone to the pub with them the night before or you spent the weekend at the hotel swimming pool. It was the ultimate 'expat' life reminiscent of the British Raj. Often, if you were a couple, it helped if you were in different organizations working in the same environment because, inevitably, your organizations would work with each other, which would be a tacit form of support. I heard of one story of an American agency funding another French agency in the east of Sri Lanka, where the husband worked for the former in the capital and the wife worked for the latter. It certainly made interesting anecdotes about per diems and travel. Sri Lanka is not that big, and working in the tsunami and conflict region is even more limited, so you end up working in this incestuous small space.

Part of the White privilege ironically can be seen from the White SUV. This was brought home to me one day, making a field trip to the northeast of Sri Lanka during the conflict. We didn't have a vehicle nor felt there was a need for one because of the need to conserve our finances, so we hired a taxi to take us. We were stopped by the army and asked about our movements. When we showed them our registration as an NGO, we were asked why we didn't have our own SUV with the logo and flag of our organization prominently displayed on the side. Thinking that we needed to work locally and not be seen as ostentatious, we were made to realize that this was what was needed for us to work properly in conflict areas of Sri Lanka and to be taken seriously.

The White SUV is symptomatic of a privilege that NGOs feel, providing them protection from the outside with their logo, their flag and other accessories. In many parts of the world, this SUV is also bulletproof. It symbolizes the difference between the international staff and the local community. The air conditioning, satellite radio system and other fancy toys that these SUVs are specially equipped with are different from the transport of the local community who use public transport and have to suffer local checkpoints and other inconveniences that the White SUV overcomes.

Imagine a queue at a military checkpoint where a bus has stopped, and locals come out to get their things checked. A White Toyota SUV pulls up behind the bus and promptly moves toward the checkpoint. A pass is shown, and the SUV is waved through. At certain times, local staff is co-opted into this space when the internationals deploy to the field for 'missions'. Only then are they 'rewarded' with the same protection. However, once this mission is over, the local staff will revert to being local. The symbol of the White man or woman sitting in front of the Black driver is the image of the NGO worker heroically coming to save the day. Thus, the White SUV somehow ironically represents White privilege, literally and figuratively. The White SUV represented a sense of false protection that people felt that if you were in this with your logo, you would be identifiable by parties to the conflict and not targeted. However, as recent sad incidents have shown us, these perceptions of protection have been misguided as many more are now targeted. I, of course, chose to go with a green SUV made in India to buck this trend.

LESSON IN POWER AND PRIVILEGE

In hindsight, my experience of the humanitarian community in 2005 in Sri Lanka was a massive lesson in power and privilege and definitely reminiscent of colonial times gone by. From the White 4-wheel drives parked outside 5-star hotels to the parties to the jackets, logos and coordination meetings, it was clear that you had to be part of the system. It turned out for me that you had to be the right color, age and gender and move in the right circles. You needed to be in the right crowd granting you access to the right knowledge and information. You were valued not for the expertise and experience you had but more for the connections you made.

So what have I learned from these incidents? The realization is that this industry has a bias towards people of color. There are lingering remnants of colonialism visible in aid flows through humanitarian systems shaped exclusively by Western / Christian values seeking to change the social, political and economic structures of countries in the Global South with little input from affected communities. For many in the international sector, the system of humanitarian action suffers from a deep systemic problem of asymmetric power that comes from a pedagogy that Brown and Black subjects are not ready to take control of their destiny.

The current system is the grandchild of the colonial missionaries and is a result of the hangover of colonialism. This colonial legacy has been reformed in the systems and structures that 'civilizing missions' and humanitarian agencies from the colonial powers still perpetuate. Much of the contemporary laws, policies and actions instituted in and by humanitarian and development organizations often reinforce the colonial power dynamics of people and institutions from the Global North systemically oppressing and exercising domination over those from the Global South. It is these legacies influencing humanitarian assistance and development activities that affected people often feel that the services provided for them are not designed with their input and according to their needs. It is these legacies that influence how affected people are treated and described, essentializing a level of dependency and a lack of agency to them. I felt it on the ground from both those who perpetuated the system and those who somehow benefited from it.

We need to break the White gaze in international development and humanitarian action by questioning whose expertise we value, whom we listen to, who holds the levers of power and who gets a vote. We need to dismantle how we construct the communities we work in as the 'other', i.e., places overseas with problems and needs, rather than places where solutions are generated, and capabilities are in place. This starts with being humble about who we are and how we go about things.

12

Macaulayputras and the 'Brown Saviors' in the World Bank's Advisory Services: A Story[1]

Anonymous 2

*We must at present do our best to form a class
who may be interpreters between us and
the millions whom we govern, a class of persons
Indian in blood and colour, but English in tastes,
in opinions, in morals and in intellect*
–Lord Thomas Babington Macaulay, 1835

This personal narrative derives from spending over half a decade at the International Finance Corporation-World Bank's Advisory Services' field offices. I argue that terms such as White Savior and 'carpet bagger' are as dated as colonial regimes. Rather, I problematize the measures of the 'Brown Saviors', an emerging mid-level manager class in the aid bureaucracy through whom the ghosts of White Saviors remain alive. The first-hand observations reveal that Brown

---

[1] This short story employs the techniques of fiction to retell the true, inner practices of the international development industry. While none of the characters portrayed in the story are real-life persons, much of the content illustrated is re-imagined and simplified from real-life scenarios. Since it is a story, I also felt obliged to use my imagination as it deemed necessary.

Saviors are born and raised in South Asia, educated and indoctrinated in Macaulayism (the policy of introducing the English education system to British colonies), and employ cultural currency to earn administrative trust from the 'White masters' in the headquarters to run field operations. Through several reflections, this narrative exposes that Macaulayputras (followers of Macaulayism) in the aid industry quite often operate like the *hawaldars* (sergeants) of the East India Company to deliver 'development' results. At the same time, Macaulayputras appear to favour White aid administrators with extra privileges but subjugate most Brown subordinates and discriminate against Brown staff, service providers and clients according to the social scale of class, while with a sole purpose to advance within the aid hierarchy.

GULSHAN I, DHAKA, 2007

Country Manager Amit Arora and Deputy Country Manager Pradeep Karki–two powerful grand masters of the international aid game–sat across each other on leather sofas inside Amit's well-decorated office. Two China cups and saucers were neatly placed on a tray on a coffee table in between. To an untrained eye, they were mirror reflections of each other based on some common ground–each claimed credit for the development of typhoons happening in Bangladesh. Leaning back on the lush sofas, they acted relaxed and discussed things that seemed pressing–the latest and upcoming trips, politics, new business books, houses in Bethesda and common acquaintances getting divorced and remarried.

But an uneasiness kept brewing inside Pradeep. If the quintessential trait of a seasoned bureaucrat was to talk at ease without providing the slightest trace of what's in his mind and, thus, produce a tensed air around, Amit Arora with his English accent authored that manual, or so Pradeep thought. He leaned forward to pour tea and clutched the teapot in both hands, one for the pot and the other one to keep the lid from falling off. Once he finished nursing the teapot and tenderly placed a cup in front of his Indian boss, Pradeep relaxed his shoulders and briefly looked around. Amit's office was designed to smack his visitors with a powerful right hook. Power radiated from the massive Persian rug, leather sofa sets and ancient mahogany desk. There was power too in the array of electronic gadgets, including the latest Blackberry at his disposal. The flamboyant abstract paintings by local celebrity artists and dark bookshelf displaying corporate heavyweights such as *Lean Six Sigma, Execution, Long Tail* and the latest *Economist* sealed the deal. All courtesy of the World Bank and its poverty reduction campaign in Bangladesh.

Amit enjoyed the essence of Assamese bergamot oil in the Earl Grey tea and took a cautious sip while appraising the sly fox sitting across. He had just learned that Pradeep would like to hire a Bangladeshi to develop a sophisticated system for monitoring and evaluation (M&E). Since his expat Nepalese deputy did nothing without an ulterior motive, Amit felt the pressing need to have another off-the-record conversation with the HR coordinator, who proved to be handy in disclosing intel.

'I saw your candidate's CV', Amit concealed a sigh. 'Is your candidate ambitious?' Amit asked with a tone of frank distaste.

Judging by Amit's crystal stare, Pradeep smiled mischievously but replied flatly, 'What I gather is he is a scorpion; he's intelligent; he'd better be ambitious.'

Pradeep added nonchalantly, 'Intelligence without ambition is a bird without wings.'

Amit placed the thumb and forefinger of his right hand on the bridge of his nose to adjust its position. A moment of silence bought him the time to compose his argument.

'Do you happen to know the difference between a quail and a crane?'

'Enlighten me, please.' Pradeep anticipated a deflection, typical of Amit.

'Well, although both quail and crane can be found in the Himalayas, only the crane can fly across the Himalayas. That context is important here, Pradeep', Amit sneered, 'You have been with us for several years now.'

Amit frequently reminded Pradeep he was an outsider and that it was Amit who had given Pradeep the opportunity to the Ivy League World of the World Bank from the bush league Non-Governmental Organizations (NGOs). How Pradeep managed to contemplate the sight and maintain his composure, he did not know, but he swallowed the slap silently and kept on looking. By some bitter inner discipline, he also kept his lips tightly closed.

Amit continued as if he was a professor speaking to his newly recruited graduate student, 'Are you aware of how the President of the World Bank and the Secretary-General at the United Nations are picked for their jobs?'

'I am listening,' said Pradeep hiding his sigh. This is what happens when you work for an insecure wrinkly man that likes to moan. But Pradeep tried his best to appear attentive to his boss.

'Ideally, for the selection committee members, the obvious conclusion is that the contest for United Nations Secretary-General is neither about vision nor about the best resume, nor language skills, nor administrative ability, nor even personal charisma,' Amit paused. 'It is a political decision, made

187

principally by the five most powerful countries at the United Nations with veto power. The system prefers the least objectionable candidate.' Amit said in requiem mode.

'The position for the Bangladeshi candidate at discussion is not a big deal, Amit. You are scaring me.' Pradeep's lips upturned into a mischievous smile as he emptied the rest of his cup. Then shook his head. 'Managing a kid should not be an issue.'

'I need to flag one more concern, Pradeep,' said Amit proudly, as if he was in a must-win debate.

Feeling the need for a stimulant, Pradeep closed his eyes and imagined having a double shot of espresso and said dryly, 'Sure, I am listening.'

Pradeep met Amit's gaze. His eyes were chestnut brown and shinier than usual. Amit took a cautious sip and resumed, 'Don't you think it would have been better if we asked Washington to send us a consultant to get the advertised job done? I am sure you won't disagree that Washington has the ultimate say in everything we do. So, I must insist you hire a known *gora* (White) consultant from the Bank's consultant roster.'

A vibrating noise on Amit's Blackberry interrupts his words. Pradeep was about to stand up and fetch it from the bookshelf where it was being charged. But Amit gestured to him to stay seated and said, 'Eventually, you will need to sell your Monitoring and Evaluation system to Washington for buy-in and endorsement. So, let me ask you a simple question, Pradeep. Could you sell a posh Rolex without its certificate?'

Pradeep exhaled, appearing patient. 'I understand your concern, Amit'. He hid a sigh. 'Yes, *gora* United States citizens, British consultants perform all our technical tasks. But the practice is problematic.' Pradeep breathed in to get ready for a longer explanation. 'With all the important jobs done by these foreigners, there is no knowledge transfer on the ground. No doubt that our European donors and Washington are happy with the current business model, but don't you think it is about time we create a local supply pool and leverage the local potential?'

Amit felt like canceling his deputy with as much care as a blacksmith hammering a hobnail. But he hid that urge and nodded his head and said, 'Correct,' to offer approval.

Pradeep noticed his boss said 'correct' a lot, particularly when he wished to conceal his agreement or disagreement on a matter while retaining a position of authority. But Pradeep could not care less.

He added, 'I understand the merit of your insight, Amit. But if you do not act on my recommendation to go ahead with this hire, I hope you will put that in writing and remember that we had this discussion.' Pradeep paused to breathe away his irritation and quickly resumed, 'In my next performance evaluation, as you are well aware, knowledge transfer and local capacity development are two core areas of my job description.' Pradeep stopped. He had Amit, finally, in a knot. He smiled so broadly that his good humor became a disturbing element to Amit, but again Pradeep could not care any less.

'Fair enough, Pradeep.' Amit leaned back on his sofa, singling a retreat. Then, he leaned forward again, offering a solution, 'Prevention is better than cure, though. I still would recommend picking the son of the Honourable Bangladeshi Ambassador to Germany. I spoke to His Excellency this morning, and it seems like he is well-connected with the higher-ups within the country's bureaucracy. Once his son is on our payroll, getting things done in Bangladesh will become easier. You can give the "Ambassador Junior" a cosmetic role to play for a few years and bring consultants from Washington, even from Delhi.' Amit stood up and walked to the bookshelf to pick up his phone, indicating the meeting had adjourned.

The following morning, when his boss was en route to the airport to attend a meeting with the regional director in Delhi, Pradeep went for his usual 360-degree tour on the office floor. On such rounds, Pradeep carried out a Spartan-style but subtle inspection. Considering the sophistication, resources and sensitivity of the World Bank, Pradeep believed it was imperative to keep his Bangladeshi staff on a leash. If anything went south at the office, it was Pradeep who had to answer and explain matters to asshole Amit Arora and his cronies in Delhi and Washington. Pradeep wished to avoid that at any cost.

For good measure, Pradeep also kept an open-door policy. He wanted to be perceived as easily accessible. It was important to keep that persona, given the presence of the White consultants from Europe and the United States that were part of the senior management's inner circles. 'Those carpetbaggers,' Pradeep murmured. Little do they acknowledge that in a country that was colonized for a long time and where corporate culture was new, a class made of peasants, bureaucrats and politicians became the new super-rich to dominate the course of the privatization process to complement the bank's business model. The few with wealth, super-rich Bangladeshis, with the distilled essence of boredom from having too much, wanted even more. Unsurprisingly, the members of this social group treated the World Bank as a cash cow, and Amit and Pradeep were their 'friends' with insider knowledge of the bank's 'n' number of unguarded passages to local contracts and consultancies. Amit and Pradeep also needed these elites to tread in Dhaka's high society. Accepting their children as highly-paid World Bank interns was part of Amit and Pradeep's survival mechanism in Dhaka.

But Pradeep could barely tolerate these interns. They were generally fearless, and gossipy and treated placements at the World Bank as part of social entitlement, along with their English-medium education and bachelor's degrees from North American or British universities–quite often from second and third-tier institutions. These placeholder interns treated the office floor as a mobile fashion parade, radiating an aura that they were doing Pradeep and the whole of Bangladesh a favor by being at the World Bank. While at work, a few interns cut their milk teeth and read Stardust or Mirror magazine, others searched for potential future friends on Facebook and complained about their waistlines after being ferried about by chauffeurs and having servants carry out all their household chores. The rest of the group appeared to overcome their elephantine flat-footedness by opening an old spreadsheet or pretending to read an old memo.

Beyond the interns, the group of analysts also mainly represented the local elite families. Pradeep could name the daughter of a Supreme Court judge, the daughter of the Governor of the Central Bank, the Air Force Chief's son, the Cabinet Secretary's son and the Finance Minister's niece. These strings worked as catalysts and helped to move files and provided smooth access to the local bureaucracy. Distasteful as it may be, this was how international development had to work in Bangladesh, and it was Pradeep's job, in Amit's absence, to keep the sludge moving to secure the World Bank's poverty reduction business in the country. After all, he was not paying the salaries to the scions of power out of his own pocket; and the taxpayers in the rich countries who fund this whole business would never know what went on in the field offices. As Pradeep had observed during his 30 years in poverty reduction, this practice was the norm. I worked hard to find a different answer, but all I got to show was my blistered feet. So, Pradeep kept his enemies close and enjoyed the entitlements—tax-free booze and fat hardship allowances. And everything's fine as long as Washington is content.

The entitled interns and analysts in the office blissfully coexisted by an abstract iron curtain with the job-fearing, hard-working middle-class people, who, predictably, maintained their 'prisoner on parole' attitude as their social standing depended on keeping their jobs intact. Frequently concerned about their yearly contracts not being renewed and fear of missing out on a fat World Bank pension and perks, the middle-class staff office members usually kept their heads down and did what Pradeep told them to do. His open-door policy could not melt the distance these people wanted to maintain physically and emotionally. Ironically, Pradeep again realized that's how the World Bank operated in Bangladesh.

Pradeep once jokingly toyed with Amit to consider changing that operating model. He wanted to meaningfully engage the interns in long-term projects and teach them professionalism. But Amit punctured that wishful thinking by panicking instantly, 'Sweep that expectation under the carpet, my advice,' were his exact words. Amit explained he needed all Bangladeshis at his office precisely for what chefs use herbs for —to subtly keep them in the background to enhance the flavour of the main dish—poverty reduction through private sector development, as long as Washington kept sending the necessary skills and technical expertise to get things done. Pradeep often referred to this practice by Amit as 'Amit-vellian'. But Amit couldn't care less.

Pradeep stared at a wall painting in his office by famous Bangladeshi painter Shahabuddin Ahmed depicting Bengali dynamism through fearless human figures navigating the hardships of life. Pradeep mischievously grinned at the irony of Ahmed's misplaced optimism.

REFERENCES

Macaulay, T.B. (1919) 'Minute on Education', in Sharp, H. (ed) *Selections From Educational Records, Part I (1781-1839),* Calcutta, Bureau of Education, Superintendent, Government Printing

13

'H' is for Heroes With Hologram Haloes: A Testimony of Saviorism and Ministry

Chongo Beverly Anne Mwila

Nearly a decade ago, I worked for a Christian Non-Governmental Organization (NGO) founded in the United States that specialized in child sponsorship. Heaven's Heroes* recruited individual donors (or a family) to sponsor the education of a child at one of two community schools in Zambia. These schools are usually primary / elementary school level establishments that typically cater to the most disadvantaged families, i.e., those who cannot even afford the 'free' government schools because of the high cost of user fees. In addition to covering school fees, assistance was rendered to providing midday meals and addressing their health needs. The organization also had a children's home where the extremely vulnerable children were placed under their guardianship and care.

When I first stumbled upon them, it was this incredibly noble-sounding work that made me eager to use my experience in education and development to contribute to their efforts. However, this eagerness was coloured by anxiety when I discovered that neither of the two ladies in charge had education or child protection qualifications; 'The Founder' headed the United States office and was a professional photographer, and 'The Director' in charge of in-country operations was a trained soprano. Sure, the latter had supposedly previously facilitated some adoptions, but it hardly seemed enough to warrant entrusting her with a handful of children. In fact, in their own country, I daresay their lack of professional training would have raised enough red flags for authorities. Here, however–in a so-called Christian nation that I often describe as having a 'colonial hangover'–all they needed was the 'right' colour skin and an inflated sense of self heavily doused in righteousness.

During the initial orientation / indoctrination period, I often heard about how the impetus for these angels' good deeds was their desire to counteract the villainy of another NGO founded in the United States, the Jesus Crusaders.[1] Apparently, Jesus Crusaders had presented themselves as nothing short of a gift from God lovingly given to the poor Zambian people. They had ingratiated themselves with the government and influential members of society, all the while carrying out nefarious profit-making schemes which supposedly included some dubious adoptions and the liberal use of the truth (complete with staging photos to exaggerate the circumstances of some children) to recruit new donors. The benevolent United States nationals who funded the operations were blissfully ignorant and some pensioners allegedly incurred financial hardship (including losing their homes) in an effort to donate. It was shocking stuff, but I would soon learn that the ones judging them were not exactly innocent. In fact, it only took about three months before I realized that for all their preaching and holiness, the Heroes' operations were also often questionable and problematic.

---

[1] Not real names

My discussion of the questionable and problematic operations begins with the donors. Although I would like to believe that the first appeals that the organization did were honest in their presentation of the children's situations, by the time I was leaving, I had noticed a pattern emerging of embellishing the children's pasts, a practice that felt exploitative of everyone involved. For example, I distinctly remember there being interest in getting an albino child, perhaps because his / her story could be told against the backdrop of the ritual killings and other terrible things that are caused, in part, by othering those born with Albinism.

I also remember the story of two siblings, Eliza and Samson,[2] where it was insinuated that they were orphans who had been living unsupervised, and then had been separated. Our quest–with the generous help of a few donors–was to reunite them. However, the truth was that although the home situation was not ideal, their widowed mother was alive, and we were the ones that separated them when we first decided to take Eliza. The real motive for taking Samson in was his intelligence, and therefore, his potential to be an academic Heroes success story.

When a successful campaign resulted in the siblings being reunited, further donations were solicited to help get Samson set up. School supplies like bags and stationery were already available, so the biggest expense was his clothing. A conservative estimate of what was raised would be $200. Instead of giving us the amount in its entirety so that new clothes could be purchased, a House Mother and I received a sliver of the money and were sent to scrounge around for what –with prices in the two Zambian kwacha per item range (about 12 cents at today's rate)–were surely third-hand clothes. In

2 Not real names.

contrast to this tight-fisted behaviour with Samson, was the relative ease with which the organization overpaid for a car bought from the director's brother-in-law; an impractical vehicle that was expensive to maintain and always breaking down.

Unfortunately, there was not much I could do or say about either situation. Over time I had learnt that although my title suggested clout, I did not have any power. I could not even express my worry that as great as the reunion of the siblings was, it increased the risk of a disease outbreak triggered by the Home's challenge with running water. Additionally, there had been other issues that made me reluctant to bring another child in. For instance, the continued stay of a House Mother who the children reported meted out excessive corporal punishment and whose repeated theft from the house coffers often caused supply shortages. There was also the alleged molestation of some of the younger girls by the older boys, but I am reluctant to dwell on that because I never actually heard any of the girls accuse their 'siblings'. I only know what the director felt it necessary to tell me, the fact that two boys (including one who was HIV positive) were then removed from the Home, and that eventually there was a counsellor who started coming in to speak to the children. I had broached the subject of reporting the allegations to the Department of Social Welfare, but not surprisingly, that was brushed aside.

Apart from the Home, this insistence on doing things a certain way was also evident in how Heaven's Heroes interacted with the community schools. The decidedly asymmetrical relationship was often emphasized in the 'it's our way or the highway' attitudes of the founder and the director. One of the ways that manifested was when they resolved to bring in a new headteacher to one of the schools. All the recruitment procedures were done by us, and if I recall correctly, the owner-cum-headteacher of the school only met the successful candidate once, shortly before we confirmed his appointment. A few years ago, I learnt how this same school had almost shut down because when Heaven's Heroes basically decided to pivot from supporting the schools to actively competing against them, they had spirited all the children who had been in sponsorship away, which–thanks to an aggressive sponsorship drive a few years before–was nearly all the children from kindergarten to the seventh grade enrolled in the school.

That hardly seems like the behaviour you would expect from people who described their work as 'ministry', and yet it was the sort of behaviour I saw repeatedly. Unhappy though it made me, I stayed because I was advised that it would not look good to create a gap in my curriculum vitae if I could avoid it. So, I stayed and bided my time waiting another 20 months before I gave notice. Incidentally, it was around that time that new in-country or local staff contracts had been presented. Unlike the previous two-year contracts, these were one-year contracts that, despite the rising cost of living, had negligible salary increments and terrible conditions. The organization had decided, for example, that although they were legally obligated to provide gratuity at the end of the contract, they would dispense it depending on performance. Furthermore, it would not be the 25 per cent that was acceptable at the time, instead it would be whatever they saw fit including absolutely nothing. None of that made sense to my co-workers and I when we discussed it, and (coupled with all the other reasons) it actually validated my decision to leave.

Although some of my colleagues had expressed dissatisfaction to me even before the new contracts were presented, they had also expressed feelings of despondency because their educational qualifications (the majority of them had ninth- and twelfth-grade certificates) somewhat limited their employment options. Although I initially thought it was wonderful of the Heroes to employ people based not merely on qualifications but on their desire to improve children's lives, I later started to wonder if it was not a deliberate ploy for manipulation and control. Indeed, though unprovoked, there were always the explicit ways of asking 'Why would you leave?' but also the implicit 'And where would you go?' as though the Heroes were the only ones who would ever give them a chance. Having given you a chance, you were expected to be grateful and loyal. Choosing to leave declared I was neither of those things, and the vitriolic response said as much. For about a week, I was lambasted non-stop by the founder via WhatsApp messages questioning my sanity, my decision-making, berating me, belittling my intelligence and more. It was all the more jarring because this was someone who was always saying she loved and prayed for me.

I had a similarly jarring experience recently when I went on the Heroes' website and could not find a trace of the two community schools that had essentially provided the foundation for the organization. It was as if they had never existed. Although the organization is still providing education as it said it would (and perhaps this is what helped with whatever story it told donors to justify its actions), it seems dishonest and wrong not to acknowledge that current efforts were made possible by milking those already disenfranchised community schools. In fact, a cynic might suggest that perhaps the plan all along was to use the two schools–try out classroom design, fine-tune the sponsorship process, practice teacher recruitment, gauge how to balance increased enrolment with meal planning–as a means to this exact end, i.e., setting up their own school. In Bemba, we say, *ichikupempula echikulya* which literally translates as 'the thing

199

that visits you is the one that eats you.' Simply put, it is a caution to beware of whom you keep close to, and one that, rather ironically, has many biblical parallels. Whether the Heroes always intended to take advantage of the schools or a plan emerged as the situation evolved, the result remains the same. I cannot help but pity the schools because the few initial benefits they accrued were not worth the suffering they endured in the end.

While the schools were visibly absent, something or someone who was almost overly present on the website was a young albino girl. Seeing her saddened me and reminded me that while it may indeed be considered a blessing when these 'Good Samaritan' organizations offer to help our communities, there is a need to proceed cautiously, both at the individual school level and at the national level. In the Zambian context, for instance, I strongly believe there is a need for either the Ministries of Education or Community Development, respectively, to step in to formalize and regulate relationships between organizations like Heroes and schools. That way, even if the relationship sours, there is some recourse or an established way to dissolve the partnership. Additionally, while I understand the human resource constraints, there definitely needs to be better monitoring of the places where children are taken into temporary care. Over the course of two years, I only participated in one pre-arranged, a highly controlled visit, which did not involve seeing or interviewing the children. To this day, that continues to strike me as odd and possibly even negligent, no matter how much faith those welfare officers had that the children were well taken care of.

14

The 'Local' and White Saviorism in the Caribbean

Jody-Ann Anderson

THE WEIGHT OF SILENCE AND
THE COURAGE TO SPEAK

W hen I saw the call for testimonies about White Saviorism in international development, I hesitated. I hesitated not because I did not have a valid contribution to make but because I have witnessed, over the years, what happens to those who speak up, particularly those who are not in positions of privilege. Besides, I learned early on that silence could be the difference between life and death: walk and live, talk and die.

The rhetoric around silence was only reinforced once I entered the workforce, as people who expressed opposition to dominant norms are frequently considered difficult or 'not a team player'. Therefore, I experienced a constant tension between my professional and, in some cases, physical survival and my commitment to work towards social change purposefully. Yet, as a Ph.D. candidate with years of experience in the 'field', I am aware of the privilege I have to add my voice to a serious piece of scholarship that provides alternate perspectives to dominant narratives currently existing in the international development discourse and practice. Also, as a person who identifies with several intersecting marginalized groups, I am conscious of the power that comes with telling my story—reclaiming my truth. Therefore, I welcome the reader to journey with me through this discovery process, not as a companion, but as an active participant who viscerally experiences the words I have written, to unveil the forms of White superiority that I experienced and their persistence in international development.

THE LURE OF THE INTERNATIONAL
AND A HOPE FOR STABILITY

I can still remember the day that I got the job. After a few years of working in the local Non-Governmental Organization (NGO) sector in the Caribbean, being overworked as I bounced between several projects as a means of stringing together enough funds to earn a living wage, I was ready for a change that could advance me towards my professional and personal goals. I had great expectations when I landed the role of a 'local' programme officer (later changed to programme manager) with an International NGO (INGO) seeking to make a difference in the lives of the poor and vulnerable through its humanitarian work. My hopes were primarily tied to beliefs that an INGO would be better placed to provide job security, professional growth and similar guarantees that one considers when looking for employment, essentially what the local NGO could not offer. This belief is tied to common knowledge that INGOs are often better funded, given their ability to access pools of resources that are out of reach of local organizations in 'developing' countries. Many are headquartered in 'developed' countries and have long histories of 'doing development' primarily abroad while managing large funding volumes generated through grants and private donations. These kinds of experiences are privileged by major donors when making funding decisions, which means that INGOs are often better positioned to pursue and capitalize on these funding opportunities. Complementarily, country exclusions and other complex requirements limit and, in many cases, inhibit local organizations from accessing these lucrative funding streams directly.

Consequently, while local NGOs are often relied on to spearhead activities on the ground, it is usually in the capacity of implementing 'partners' and not direct grant recipients, which has many overt and covert implications. Therefore, as a 'local' development professional in a 'developing' country, working for an INGO or a multilateral institution becomes the gold standard for employment in the sector. It was what many of my colleagues in the field hoped for; it was what I hoped for –a proverbial foot in the door of the larger development machinery.

SAVIORISM, REPRESENTATION AND
TICKING ALL THE RIGHT BOXES

I embraced my new role with enthusiasm and vigor and aimed to make use of an opportunity I had worked tirelessly for. I became even more intrigued as I learned more about the work that focused on local solutions to a common problem in some marginalized neighborhoods in the region. On paper, the project ticked all the boxes of local ownership, local solution, local partners and now, with me being hired, a local staff. Therefore, White Saviorism or even notions of White superiority were not terms that instantly came to mind during my initial reflections about this experience, given the emphasis on the local and the 'empowerment' of community members to create their solutions.

Indeed, White Saviorism is often connected to a mentality where external actors (normally Caucasians, from 'developed' countries) believe they have or might I say are the solution to many of the difficulties faced by marginalized groups in contexts classified as 'developing'. Truly, except for a few colleagues, most of the expats I worked with or met appeared sincerely interested in making a difference in the lives of the people we served. Therefore, my experience with White Saviorism in international development should not be viewed through a microlens that focuses on the individual or aspects of intentionality. Doing so would feed into the misperception that those complicit in perpetuating White Saviorism are morally flawed and intentional in their actions. Many times, this is not so. Thus, it is not about an individual's goodness (or lack thereof) or their intent. Instead, a systemic lens is needed to view the complex web of social and political structures that privilege Whiteness and perpetuate the structural marginalization of groups based on characteristics like race, gender and citizenship. As such, White Saviorism entails more than representation, as this results in the issue being condensed into a tick-box exercise. By doing so, we mask deeper dynamics and institutional structures that are more subtle but just as lethal and destructive–structures that privilege Whiteness, privilege the external and privilege the 'developed'.

POWER RELATIONS, THE PURSE STRING AND APPEASING THE WHITE SAVIOR

To understand the structures and dynamics of privilege, it is crucial that we examine the power relations between locals and INGOs, who holds power, who makes the important decisions, who controls funding allocation and so forth. While the growing emphasis on local representation gives the appearance of equality and power-sharing, locals and INGOs remain aware of where power truly lies. As the familiar adage says, 'those who control the purse string make the rules'.

As stated earlier, many INGOs have greater access to funding streams. They are often the primary grant recipients, which means they are the ones setting the agenda, controlling budgetary allocations and in direct contact with donors. Therefore, although local partners are often asked to draft their budget, it must fit within the ceiling determined by the INGO, even if this means unrealistic personnel, administrative and project expenses. In these instances, the space for serious negotiation is limited, and partners often must 'make it work' for fear of losing a source of funding in contexts with limited alternatives. In contrast, while INGOs must also abide by donor funding caps, their more diverse funding streams afford greater flexibility to negotiate. They frequently have flat overhead percentages and set salary scales built into the many projects they manage. Thus, it is commonplace in 'developing' countries for power to be skewed in the INGOs' favor, which feeds into long-standing structures of superiority and inferiority and of savior and victim.

Elements of this unequal system may present themselves in less overt forms. I recall shadowing an expat colleague of different color, gender and citizenship during the early days of my employment. In discussions, they painted an idealistic picture of the main project, including the organizations' relationship with stakeholders, and attributed challenges to the difficulties of remote project oversight. While I agreed that the project had merits and was innovative, internally, I had misgivings about how I would be received, given my social location. Because being 'local' meant that I had extensive knowledge of the context's patriarchal legacies and societal divisions based on class and shade. However, since I was warmly received by those I met as we made the rounds during the orientation and handover process, even sharing meals with some people of influence, I hid my hesitations.

The validity of my initial apprehensions was confirmed afterward when I was on my own executing the tasks of my job description. For example, as a strategy to relaunch project activities that had stalled due to various factors, I approached a person of influence locally to solicit their support for work being done in a violent, marginalized neighborhood. While they agreed to the meeting, it quickly became evident that my conversation with this person was pointless–it would get me nowhere. As I spoke, I recall them laughing in disdain as if to say, 'who do you think you are to approach me!' This experience contrasts significantly with the times my Caucasian colleague(s) from the INGO visited (even those of a comparable professional level), and I made similar requests. Like magic, people were more cooperative and rolled out the proverbial red carpet. It was as though the presence of Whiteness was an automatic key to gaining access, an almost guaranteed willingness to collaborate.

As I reflect, I recognize that the disparity between how I was treated by my compatriots when I was on my own, compared to when my expat colleagues visited, is connected to persisting notions of Whiteness as being superior even in, and maybe more so in, 'developing countries' that are still grappling with the effects of colonialism. Embedded in these dynamics are the unspoken yet understood and accepted knowledge that in international organizations, including INGOs like where I worked, power-holders are often from historically privileged groups. Even when there are local offices, it is often understood that key decisions are not made by 'local' staff but 'international' ones, those who 'fly in' or the anonymous saviors based in regional offices or headquarters. Thus, in contexts of scarce resources, some locals may embody the role of victim to play a system that is only responsive to them in this role and look to and embrace the White Savior for the potential benefits that can be derived. Because, while local staff may share the INGOs identity on paper, it is often quite clear that traditional power relations remain, and that Whiteness continues to be superior.

OBVIOUS SECRETS AND
THE MAINTENANCE OF INEQUALITY

Inequality between the local and the international is also maintained by internal action and inaction, both overt and subtle, which persistently feed into patterns of differences and otherness. Many of these practices are widespread in the employment procedures of international development organizations and can easily be overlooked as standard protocols. One such example is that as local staff, I was not allowed to use the company's vehicle during my travels to project implementation sites, even those that were several hours away. It would have been fine if this was standard practice for all staff members, but before my employment, my expat colleague had access to the company vehicle when they visited. In fact, they were the only staff at the time, so it would be fair to say that the company vehicle was procured for their use. Even after I came on board, they still had exclusive use of the company vehicle during their visits. Partners and participants would know my colleague was in-country because that would be the only time that I rode in the company's vehicle. While I received an allowance for traveling, I could not understand what made it okay for my international White colleague (in a similar role) to have access to a tool to do the job. In contrast, I, a local person of color with capacity, did not. While there may be reasonable justifications, someone conscious of anti-oppressive practices would have been aware of what this seemingly small difference communicates and how it feeds into historical structures of power and inequality.

Other disparities between local staff and expats reinforced the narrative of the superiority of Whiteness. During my tenure, I realized that my salary and benefits were significantly lower than the expat who previously held my position. The justification I was given is that local salaries are aligned with the prevailing rates in that country, while expats are paid using a separate scale for 'international' staff. I could not see this logic because both local staff and expats lived in the same country and experienced the same cost of living. To this day, I still cannot understand why the value of my labor should be deemed less only because I am a 'national' staff. Correspondingly, international staff often receive additional benefits connected to their relocation that are generally not extended to local hires. For example, local staff often assume the risk of working in insecure contexts as part of their jobs. Yet, an expat would be entitled to perks like danger pay, thereby suggesting that localness somehow makes one impenetrable to the piercings of a bullet.

These practices are often part of the status quo and often are not questioned. Indeed, after initially flagging these issues with my supervisor, I accepted their explanation and resigned myself to the space of lesser value, and erroneously assumed that becoming an international staff would be the only way of transcending the unfair limits of being 'local'.

THE UNATTAINABLE GLASS CEILING

To surpass the professional barriers of being a local hire is no easy feat. When I was first employed, the project I assumed responsibility for was in crisis. Along with local partners, I worked assiduously to relaunch the project and ensure that all objectives were achieved within the extended timeline: an experience that remains one of my proudest professional accomplishments. The quality of my work was not only reflected in the project successes, but it was evident in the perfect evaluation that I received in my first year with the INGO and the consistently strong performance evaluations in subsequent years. Yet, despite my performance and capabilities, I remained stuck in the only role in my country of citizenship with no apparent room for growth in the organization. This was not from a lack of expressing interest to my superiors or an unwillingness to change location, or an absence of openings in the organization. Instead, there appeared to be a glass ceiling that I could not surmount as local staff. The glass ceiling was not overt or tangible, as I was not prevented from applying for openings as an external candidate would. However, while I met the education and experience requirements, I could not surmount the constraints of my citizenship. Yet, regardless of performance, expat colleagues appeared not to share this challenge, as their 'international' label seems to afford them the ability to make upward or lateral professional moves easily.

Evidence of this double standard is apparent when you consider that a former expat colleague, who previously had responsibility for the project in crisis, received a promotion and a new appointment in another country where the organization is present. This is significant because there had to be some form of mismanagement for the project to get to that state of crisis. I say this because proper project monitoring and risk management would have alerted my expat colleague to issues like cost overruns, unnecessary delays, partner staffing conflicts, etc., long before the project almost failed. The challenges, in this case, were not insurmountable and could have been remedied / avoided with good project management practices. While I am not privy to whether there was any accountability for the state of the project under their responsibility, the fact that they were promoted makes me think that there was none. Their experience contrasts significantly with the stagnation I experienced despite the strong performance in my role, which communicated a subliminal message that advancement was not based on merit and that one set of rules applies to the 'local' and another to the 'international'.

Other experiences, like the hiring of external consultants to perform tasks that I could easily be trained and permitted to do, reinforce the narrative of inferiority and otherness. It articulated that only some people were afforded higher levels of responsibilities and professional growth. For several years, despite my performance saying otherwise, I believed that it was something that I lacked that prevented me from advancing professionally in this organization. For a time, I accepted the narrative that, as local staff, I was incapable of more.

COMPLICITY AND THE PATHWAY TO CHANGE

My tipping point came when I recognized that I was repeating narratives told to me about things like salaries, benefits, etc., to partner staff. These partner staff worked long hours in very tough circumstances and were the backbone of the work we did–I know because I was there working right alongside them. Without being aware, I realized that I was becoming complicit in the very act of marginalization that I was experiencing, and unwittingly contributing to the continuation of these unequal practices and structures. This is so because as a professional, despite my frustrations and misgivings, I felt compelled to display a united front with the organization where I was employed, particularly since these are commonly 'accepted' practices. This tension undergirds the challenge of change.

The ease with which White Saviorism in international development can be perpetuated demands that we look closer at dominant practices and continuously interrogate them. Interrogation requires constantly asking who benefits and who is marginalized, as well as taking the steps necessary to eliminate the gap between the two. Given the field of development's colonial heritage, it is not enough to refer to terms like inclusion and representation without taking concrete steps to dismantle the very structures on which White Saviorism is built. A feat that requires that we all do our part consistently: one brick at a time.

15

Protecting Daughters for Gender 'Empowerment'

Radha Shah

PERIOD POSITIVE

R adha, I need you to put on your marketing hat,' said
Nazish, the founder and CEO of a social impact mobile
tech company in Islamabad, Pakistan, supported by
global aid funds. The purpose of the app the company was
creating, and for which I was a content strategist, was to
provide young women of working-class and rural socio-
economic backgrounds with access to reproductive healthcare
knowledge. The Niswaaqat app was to empower
'underprivileged girls' in Pakistan, the name itself a
portmanteau for *niswani taqat*, an Urdu translation of girl
power.

The content could be a little indirect because that would
attract the attention of state censorship and its mores around
decency. This would risk shutting down a growing start-up,
Nazish explained. I understood acutely: this was a start-up
aiming to reach a disenfranchised population, with a tiny
amount of wiggle room in a finite amount of space, propped
open by aid funds, its borders defended by liberal and left-
liberal thinkers and encroached upon by a religiously
conservative state and its brigade of populist defenders. At the

same time, educational content on topics such as puberty, periods and urinary tract infections could not be too 'bold' because that would attract the attention of parents and community leaders. Termed gatekeepers who would find such content unsavory, were seen as the primary obstacles to the widespread dispersal of the app among our target user base.

I tried to put my thinking cap on. Across such a landscape, how could we think about ways to provide young women with health-informed resources to take charge of their own socio-economic welfare? But my work kept swaying from problem-solving educational information mired in taboo to how to create and host affordable wellness infotainment. The direction was decided: 'period positive content', but without talking about your cervix. But why were we privileging power over the forms of cultural thought we were trying to change? What and where was the 'theory of change?' so dear to development discourse?

There's no shame in menstruation. Don't let periods stop you from getting an education.

'So, in this section of the article, the writer discusses tampon usage myths. Can we have a conversation?'

'Radha, you have to understand, in Pakistan ...'

Allusions to insertions were a no-go area. It was explained to me that I did not understand that underprivileged girls could not afford these products. All we needed to do was explain that periods were not a weakness and girls could go to school and play sports despite the bleeding. Certainly, the affordability of menstrual hygiene products for the working class was a problem, but that did not equate to not providing information as a solution, did it? Why were we dissuading working-class and rural women from making choices when the ability to have and make choices were exactly what defined self-empowerment?

THE EAST IS A CAREER[1]

This chapter tells my story as a gender development consultant in Pakistan researching the local implementation of internationally funded projects. As a researcher participating in strategy sessions and conducting fieldwork, I observed an adoption of White Saviorism narratives within an *ashraf* (cultural elite) savior complex. The way my employers and colleagues–often indebted to Western development funding for their careers–chose to think, make decisions and carry out their work was reflective of neo-colonial paternal discourses.

I stumbled into development because it was the closest thing to field research and long-form analytical writing at a time when the tomes of academia in Toronto felt shut to me. Islamabad was sold to me as a place full of bright, local and international professional minds–a collaborative environment for fresh, creative thinkers, many of whom wanted to do development differently. This sounded cautiously promising and an opportunity worth traveling across the world to take. 'Great for you socialist types,' said my friend Nauman, the head of corporate social responsibility at a national conglomerate.

I was not thinking of a development career as an opportunity to affect change from the inside–I did not believe in that. As a diasporic South Asian with training in post-colonial studies, I had learnt how aid economies were an extension of colonial rule. But I did believe in something else that I thought of as different, but probably was not: it might be possible to do constructive, meaningful work and build

---

[1] This title refers to Benjamin Disraeli's quote mentioned in Edward Said's *Orientalism* where he explains 'that to be interested in the East was something bright young Westerners would find to be an all-consuming passion.' (Said 1979, p. 5).

solidarities and shared understandings with different people in different fields.

On the side, I thought exploring development would be an opportunity to make some ethnographic observations about a sector I had only studied through literature reviews.

I was pleasantly surprised at first. There was a greater degree of acknowledgement and candour than I expected among international and local aid workers that development and diplomatic missions were systemically flawed. I found people like Nazish, hailed a trailblazer among young businesswomen in the country, who intimated they wanted to impact change in a locally driven way and questioned international development's proclaimed successes. But as my work with her and other organizations unfolded, I learned they were uninvested in unmooring themselves from saviors' frameworks of thought and practice and instead reinvested these in cultural modalities of protecting women's respectability.

Niswaaqat was to make articles and audio clips available in English and regional languages, animated series tackling conservative social understandings of health rights and video interviews with forward-thinking health professionals. It was to democratize access to progressive, medically sound educational information on adolescent girls' health that a cross-section of the non-elite classes could access. I wrote a concept note about how Niswaaqat's content would aim to address gaps in the health knowledge market for disenfranchised women, which Nazish approved.

I was excited. More than examining theory in praxis, this would be an immersive education opportunity for me to work with and learn from the people navigating, negotiating and resisting living and working in a developmentalist state. I started to feel like some of my disillusionment with development could be allayed through involvement at a grassroots level. Maybe there was an anti-neo-colonial movement within a locally driven social entrepreneurial sector. A segment that hoped to unencumber itself from the arithmetic of disbursement: loan amount divided by number of girls 'reached' equals success.

But the same sources of funding seed the accelerators who fund social impact organizations through public-private partnerships. The new challenge of commercial viability stymies ideation. The two are always struggling against one another: how can an app sell thought-changing ideas in a market that is familiar with and controlled by the hold of its more conservative strata? This becomes a question of risk, and I started to understand the log frame. A social idea was being justified as an economic reality: this society was not ready for progressive knowledge.

'Article three in this series covers the topic of menstrual discomfort and abdominal cramping, and explains when it's a good idea to seek medical attention.'

'We need to provide recipes for desi *totke*[2] for period pain,' interrupted Nazish.

Was Niswaaqat itself the gatekeeper, barring the door to young women from empowering themselves?

Outside the boardroom, women marched and chanted: *mera jism meri marzi*.[3]

LET GIRLS GO TO FINISHING SCHOOL

'We do this. See?' The programme manager of an internationally funded women's vocational training programme pointed to the word 'agency' in the PowerPoint

---

[2] Herbal home remedies.

[3] My body, my right.

file. In my proposal, I had posed a question about exploring how programme enrollees conceptualized the notion of agency.

The next day, she called me urgently and said I had to immediately get on a flight to interior Sindh to participate in the closing ceremonies of the programme. One of my tasks was to see what trainees had 'achieved' since its completion over a period of a few months. Had they turned their internship placements into jobs or begun their own businesses –or not?

In one classroom of a large modern boys academy that had lent its premises for the event, a presenter from a local financial inclusion-focused non-profit asked the young women to close their eyes and imagine a house, and then for one volunteer to walk the class down her imaginative path to 'realizing her potential.'

From a distance, she saw the house as a whole. As she approached, her vision zoomed in.

A house became a home, with a garden, pretty windows, frilled curtains and filled rooms.

It was a metaphorical lesson meant to convey how dreaming up and filling all the components of life was a path to becoming a complete person.

No longer a simple village girl–*jo ghar pe bethi hain*–who is sitting at home.

'They have no grooming,' said Ashraf, the community mobilizer, at dinner on the lawn of a neighbouring 'colony'. Multinational industrial organizations build onsite residential enclaves for the families of husbands posted for managerial work. The paternal language disturbed me, including its unintended but nonetheless sexualized connotation.

'They don't know how to speak or what to wear,' he said, describing the participants as uncouth country bumpkins, unfinished for employability in modern Pakistan.

His job involved convincing parents in the rural community to allow their daughters to join the training programme. Cultural hurdles, he explained, were the greatest barrier with parents not wanting girls to participate because leaving the home and mobility go against tradition. 'Culture *ijazat nahi deta ke gari mein akeli jaye*.[4] So we talked to the families and we told them we'll provide buses, and we will ensure your daughters are safe [read: remain honourable], from point A to B.'

In this way, tradition was a hurdle that would not deter development. Development would find a path around a community's 'backward' ways, even if that meant helping to reinforce a patriarchal norm that would ensure successful programme completion. At the table, there was local barbecue, Chinese food and Russian salad–the quintessential middle-class dining out experience. This was the world the girls should be aspiring to be a part of.

'As women, we think if we're four inches taller we might have a better chance of getting a job. So girls go all the way to buy a new pair of shoes, that will be so uncomfortable ke sara concentration us *cheez pe chali jayeg*,'[5] said Farah, an instructor at the partnering vocational training college. 'How much makeup should you wear? Are you supposed to wear all you jewelry? Should your nail colour be catchy–having covered this, then we move on to mock interview practice?' she continued.

---

[4] Our culture does not permit girls to travel alone in cars.

[5] They won't be able to focus on the task at hand

In my assessment, aspects of the programme taught valuable job-hunting skills, while such disciplinary rhetoric reminded trainees that feminine sexuality was a danger that was their responsibility to contain. There was a preoccupation with the idea that if girls are allowed in public, they would immediately and inadvertently attract licentious attention. So, they must be taught docility.

'What did you learn about interviewing skills in your training session,' I asked.

'You have to speak quickly. And you shouldn't take too much time to think,' responded Zahra, a trainee.

'You know, sometimes it's important to be thoughtful, that also reflects,' I attempted to interject.

'No,' she said firmly, 'You have to speak quickly because you shouldn't waste their time.'

Later, Zahra would explain that instead of a customer service role she had interviewed and qualified for, she chose to become a teacher, as this was a profession respected in the community, something she and her father discussed.

'The problem,' she said, 'is people will think where this girl is going men will be there and if I'm sitting at a customer service desk, talking to a new male customer, one after the other. No matter how much you try [to go your own way], you are part of society so that's why I turned this offer down,' Zahra understood the difference between the choices she wanted to make and the choices she had to make.

CALL ME ON MY CELL PHONE THAT CAN
ONLY MEAN ONE THING (DRAKE 2016)

'I want a series on cell phones,' Nazish demanded.
'Ok?'

'In Pakistan, you know these girls; they get text messages from unknown numbers.'

'And then they call them, and they get kidnapped.'

'Ummm?'

'So we need some articles on what could happen, and how girls need to be careful.'

So began a conversation on cyberstalking.

With great technology in the hands of poor women would come the responsibility to protect their reputation and safety. They needed to be made aware of the world of cyber stalking and the dangerous doors their smartphones would open. The girl imagined in these articles is not only sexualized, but she is also dim-witted, beguiled by male attention and could end up in the arms of a lurking predator—if she is not careful. Women were to be warned that they should look after their health, stay away from men, go to school or work and go home. Freedom was dangerous and so was fun.

'Radha, I'd like to introduce you to the new marketing manager.'

' Hi, I'm Aneesa, I'll be editing your work.'

Comparative statistics showing Pakistan is the sixth most dangerous country for women to live in, while accurate, exist in a vacuum of intersectional historical, political and economic understandings that need to be more widely available. Journalistic pieces turn to such facts, filling the contextual void with religio-cultural phrases describing Pakistani women as victims of a deeply conservative Islamic society. Together, such data and ideas comprise how a place is known as (in)explicably different.

In popular culture, aid work is therefore seen as the one way good around the world is accomplished, even if ordinary people cannot be involved in it themselves. Distrust and a sense of betrayal by the industry usually follow from

220

discovering corruption, embezzlement and sexual abuse scandals. Continuing to remain out of sight from the public eye are the micro-level operations of the development economy, through which transformative change is operationally unachievable by design.

International development organizations aim to 'empower' Brown women to 'save' themselves from oppression through employability, while local partner agencies cooperate as guardians protecting their 'honor'. This two-player game is meant to secure community permission for the participation of its daughters and ensure successful program implementation and disbursement of funds. White liberal understandings of women's freedom descend upon the field site as universal: poor women must go to work to be –and feel – self-empowered, to provide for their children and be good mothers, all the while contributing to economic development.

While improvements to Pakistan's ranking on the gender equality index are desired, community mobilizers, such as Ashraf, will only challenge patriarchal practices the East is ashamed of, and the West points out are backward. Girls' inner honor must be protected (Jalal 2007), and here the international development sector is happy to allow implementing partners to take the cultural lead following relativist principles rebranded as 'doing no harm'. In the local sphere, working-class women–beneficiaries–are depicted as requiring constant and vigilant protection from sexual exposure and interaction. Instead of providing women with resources to freely take charge of their own social welfare, their development is facilitated through a patriarchal– actual or virtual–chaperoned entryway into public and digital space. This is a path from which they are not to veer.

REFERENCES

Drake (2016) 'Hotline Bling', Track 16 *Views*, Cash Money Records, Republic Records, and Young Money Entertainment

Jalal, A. (2007) *Self and Sovereignty: Individual and Community in South Asian Islam Since 1850*, Lahore, Sang-e-Meel Publications

Metcalf, T.R. (2010) Ideologies of the Raj, Cambridge, Cambridge University Press

Said, E. (1979) Orientalism, New York, Random House

16

The White Savior Complex in International Cooperation Initiation Mandates

Eddy Michel Yao[1]

If I had to do it all over again, I would not participate in this three-month programme. To tell you the truth, I don't even see myself growing in the field anymore because I feel like we haven't contributed much. ... what we have achieved here, everyone, especially the youth here, can do it if they are mentored and have the same resources as we do.'

It was 2017 and I was overwhelmed by these words spoken by a volunteer who, like me, was participating in a three-month term in international cooperation initiation. The calmness and frankness with which they were spoken resonated within me. And although I did not totally agree with what was said, I had to recognize a part of the truth shared by many of us. Her speech raised questions in my mind about those months spent in a West African country. Even though my experience had been overall positive, my colleague's words invited me to look back critically at my first experience in the world of international cooperation as a 23-year-old born in Côte d'Ivoire but raised in Canada.

---

[1] Translated from French.

As time went by, while exchanging with other young people who had participated in this type of short-term program, I heard the same criticisms supported by anecdotes that did not leave me indifferent. Sometimes, they whispered to me like a confidence snatched after a disappointment or an understanding (or lack thereof) of certain patterns persisting in the world of international cooperation. Their experiences, combined with my own, made me realize the omnipresence and the often-hidden variations of White Saviorism at both the personal and organizational levels.

This personal level can be described as the set of experiences of individuals between the ages of 18 and 35 who take part in international cooperation initiatives of two weeks to six months. The organizational level refers to the international cooperation organizations that develop and implement these international solidarity initiation programs in partnership with organizations from the Global South. Generally speaking, in the Canadian context, the main funder of these programmes is the provincial or federal government.

Already in 2017, during my first international cooperation experience in Benin, I saw that within my cohort, different reasons had driven us to participate in the program. We, of course, were driven by altruistic values, but more individualistic reasons had pushed us to get involved. Whether it was to acquire skills, find a job, add an overseas experience to our CVs or open ourselves to cultural diversity, our initial motivations for participating in the program were mostly self-interested. Few people had put the communities of the Global South at the forefront of their minds during the pre-departure training and informal exchanges. Our experience in the field had undoubtedly been formative as it had allowed us to develop soft skills, in addition to knowing our capacities and limitations.

Nevertheless, at the end of the mandate, we needed help to measure the impact and relevance of our actions on the challenges and issues faced by the different actors in the field, i.e., the community organizations we worked with and their beneficiaries / members. Therefore, while there was no doubt that the experience had benefited us, we were not sure that we had achieved our objectives in such a short time. We were disappointed despite the few achievements because our expectations were so high and our vision of the world was utopian. These expectations had been reinforced by the trainers during the pre-departure training, where individualistic benefits were promoted, benefits that would give us, young people with little experience from the Global North, the opportunity to make a humanistic cultural exchange trip.

A MANIFESTATION OF THE NOTION OF PRIVILEGE

In 2019, at an international cooperation fair, a former participant said, 'I couldn't tell you if I had an impact on the people there, but what is certain is that I learned a lot about myself, improved many of my skills and my self-esteem'. This former participant kept talking about the benefits of the mandate on himself, leaving very little mention of his accomplishments in the field. To top it off, he mentioned the professional and personal privileges associated with short-term volunteering.

I too have experienced some of this privilege as someone who studied and grew up in Canada. In my various settings of intervention, no one questioned what I said. On the contrary, it was as if I knew everything and I was solicited for several missions in the host organization, even though it was outside my competence. I mostly knew how to impose my limits, but I remember an episode where a communication volunteer ruined the website of the host organization after being asked to update it. The volunteer, although not qualified, had been asked, in a confident way, to do so by the coordinator of the host organization, which of course, had catastrophic consequences for the organization. This episode also demonstrates that host organizations reinforce a paradigm that puts international volunteers and development workers on a pedestal compared to volunteers, or even employees, from the host country / community. Their blind trust in international volunteers paints them as people with boundless expertise. Yet, international volunteers, especially in youth placements, often have little experience and limited skills.

A PERSISTENT WESTERN LOGIC

Volunteers, although trained before their departure, often analyze the situations in the host country from a Western perspective. They propose solutions that are often not adapted to the host context, and they behave or say things that do not respect the culture of the host community. Very often, I heard comments or saw actions that were in opposition to the logic of solidarity. Some volunteers imposed their own desires and realities on the communities they worked with instead of listening to them and working with and for them. I also saw the difficulties of adaptation of some volunteers who put themselves on the margins instead of embracing the culture.

As someone from West Africa, I felt that, for these people, this short-term program came to reaffirm what we see on television about the poverty and socio-economic situation of so-called 'developing' countries. Pre-departure training and benevolence were not enough to deconstruct prejudices and stereotypes. As a result, these internships often reflect the White Saviorism that portrays the ignorance, lack of humility and permeability of young volunteers towards an environment

226

different from their own. Even if these acts are decried by all stakeholders in international cooperation, they still exist and are frequently reproduced in communities.

I remember this participant for whom gender and equality issues were very important. Once in the field, she insisted on applying it in the host community without really understanding the situation and the relationships that prevailed there. This obviously created friction in the community as her approach to these issues was inappropriate and out of step with the realities of the women whose lives she wanted to improve. Her approach was individualistic and focused on the individual freedoms of women (as it is in the West), which contradicted the community spirit favored by the women participating in the project.

My experiences, combined with the discussions, anecdotes and honest remarks, especially revealed to me the differences in perception of short-term international cooperation programs and the manifestation of the White Saviorism among young volunteers. They also raised questions about the responsibility of cooperation organizations in the omnipresence of White Saviorism within international solidarity. In my opinion, these organizations are often responsible for this White Savior feeling among their volunteers since they are the ones who recruit them, train them and accompany them throughout their international experience.

AN ORGANIZATIONAL VIEW

The Western monopoly that weighs on the universe of international cooperation is flagrant. Indeed, aid from the Global North is directed towards the Global South, reinforcing a certain idea of dependence on the one who is helped towards the one who helps. Knowing that this vertical conception of aid from the Global North to the Global South is presented to volunteers, one may wonder to what extent international solidarity does not represent, in the collective unconscious of our societies, the continuation of this civilizing mission advocated by the West for ages (Bazin *et al.*, 2010). We can also ask ourselves to what extent volunteers consciously or unconsciously reproduce the Western model in which they grew up.

Similarly, it is possible to observe during pre-departure training that the history of solidarity often begins with the arrival of the first White missionaries in the Global South for evangelization. Books on international cooperation rarely deal with the solidarity initiatives that existed in the past in other cultures with different neighboring peoples. Moreover, the notions of White privilege or the White Savior Complex are hardly or not at all addressed in the training, depending on the organizations. The West is always at the center, and Western values tend to be considered universal by international cooperation actors (Bazin *et al.*, 2010). Furthermore, the reappropriation and dissemination of Western values contribute to the standardization of practices in the world of cooperation, as well as to the submission and even exclusion of actors in the Global South.

Finally, a feeling of non-reciprocity between the Global North and the Global South persists. One of its manifestations is that few, if any, young people from the Global South participate in international solidarity mandates in the Global North. Some will obviously blame the lack of means or of organization, but in a logic of solidarity, of capacity building, shouldn't we look at this issue to reduce this asymmetry? If we want to create global citizens, shouldn't they come from different places, not just from the Global North? In light of these questions and of my reflections, cooperation mandates benefit volunteers from the Global North and International Organizations more than actors from the Global South (beneficiaries and host organizations).

CONCLUSION

Some of the young people participating in the international cooperation initiation mandates come back with mixed feelings about their experiences abroad. These short-term stays contain many of the characteristics of White Saviorism. Even as an individual able to identify them in an international context, it is still difficult to address the subject with the main stakeholders, i.e., the volunteers and the international cooperation organizations. The former often perceive it as a personal criticism of their professional abilities, while the latter are caught in a complex and bureaucratic system that conditions their actions. The lack of permeability to lessons learned in the field is indeed persistent and manifests itself in different ways across organizations.

At the same time, this White Saviorism goes beyond skin color or origin. It can be manifested by anyone and depends on many background factors, such as having grown up and been educated in one system rather than another. Therefore, a racialized person can unconsciously or involuntarily reproduce this complex in his or her interventions if he or she is not equipped to identify and deconstruct the different manifestations of White Saviorism.

Moreover, several writings have called for a de-Westernization of aid in favor of a willingness to think and carry out cooperation actions from the bottom up (Micheletti 2010). This is a possible solution that is articulated around the localization of aid to deconstruct the White Savior Complex in international cooperation. This chapter, therefore, calls for a broader reflection in favor of a balanced transformation not only of the funding mechanisms but also of the power relations between international solidarity organizations and their partners, i.e., the actors in the different countries of action. It is not only about getting out of the logic of the imperialist interests of the large Western powers but also about recognizing the agentivity of the different stakeholders. Overcoming the White Savior Complex, therefore, requires humility from volunteers, as well as a certain adaptive and cultural intelligence.

My thoughts are in line with those of Vinhas (2010), who encourages us to 'integrate that we are disruptors of balance and that it is not those we come to "help" who must adapt, but rather the other way around [translation]'. Similarly, we are not heroic saviors, and they are not miserable victims (Vinhas 2010). Rather, we are all respectful and open individuals who want to learn, discover and share in a spirit of solidarity to break the cycle of injustice and inequality.

REFERENCES

Bazin, M., Fry, A. and .Levasseu, P. (2010) 'L'aide humanitaire internationale non-gouvernementale: un monopole occidental', *Humanitaire*, https://journals.openedition.org/humanitaire/696, accessed 24 March 2022

Micheletti, P. (2010) 'Désoccidentaliser » n'est pas renoncer', *Humanitaire*, https://journals.openedition.org/humanitaire/691, accessed 24 March 2022

Vinhas, P. (2010) 'La désoccidentalisation, vue du terrain', *Humanitaire*, https://journals.openedition.org/humanitaire/708, accessed 24 March 2022

PART III

CONCLUSION

17

The Common Threads of White Saviorism

Themrise Khan and Maïka Sondarjee

As stated in the introduction to this book, and as reinforced by the testimonies and analysis presented thus far, this book identifies White Saviorism as an active collaborator in how development aid is structured, delivered and controlled. Most initiatives put forth by European and Western donors to address causes of inequality in the non-Western world thrive on the assumption that the latter cannot manage themselves and that it is only an external White Savior who can put things in order.

There is no doubt that the history of colonialism set the stage for the world today. However, the colonial era was not about White Saviorism. It was about White plunder. It was this plunder that was turned into saviorism once colonized countries eradicated most colonial rules from their countries. Therefore, simply recognizing the role that colonialism and racism have played in shaping the aid industry is not enough. As this book argues, the structures to control international development and aid currently in place feed off colonial attitudes, but they are an altogether different system of power than colonialism. While it feeds off the same mentality, the White Saviorism present in colonial times—cruel, violent and

Christian—is very different today. In modern times, it is more subtle, disguised under the ruse of 'partnership', 'collaboration' and 'cooperation'. Yet, it is far more dangerous than it ever was.

The authors in this book attempted to articulate White Saviorism through their own voices and experiences. Voices that White Saviors have chosen to silence because it threatens their existence and because it talks of emancipation and independence from their control. The various contributions have identified a series of behaviors, attitudes and philosophies exhibited by White Saviors in the context of development interventions and practices, which instead of creating a positive impact, have led to negative outcomes. Some of those outcomes directly relate to subjugating and suppressing the Global South by the Global North under the guise of international development.

To understand the complexity of White Saviorism in the development sector, this book needed to begin with the historical roots of White Saviorism, based on colonial conquest and the creation of Whiteness. It was also crucial to analyze the concept intersectionally, in all its gendered aspects. Then, most importantly, theory, practices and lived experiences were woven in to produce valid and novel knowledge. While the contributions in this book highlight several complexities and layers of control created by White Saviorism, some specific issues shine a light on and deserve greater attention in combatting White Saviorism.

ANNIHILATING INDIGENEITY

The beginning of colonial rule can also be seen as the end of Indigenous communities worldwide. As Marcelo Saavedra-Vargas details in his chapter, the coming of White colonial saviors was not for the benefit of the Indigenous populations of the so-called 'new' world. On the contrary, it was for their annihilation. With a premise like this, White Saviorism can never be seen as a positive indicator of human and social development, despite good intentions. And it isn't to this day, given the treatment meted out to the world's Indigenous populations. Canada, the United States, Australia, New Zealand and even some Western European countries with its treatment of the Roma, or Norway with the Indigenous Samí communities, still annihilate the life and histories of Indigenous groups.

The actual interests of the colonizers were ulterior in nature and only observable from the practices. Mpangala (2004, p. 4) has observed that colonial powers had 'interests of capitalist expansion in the colonies'. Colonizers saw as inherent to the success of their enterprise to 'dominate and control societies' (*Idem.*). As a result, they created ideologies of ethnicity and sociological theories based on Social Darwinism psychology, i.e., some people are less evolved than others and need civilizing to aid their evolutionary process. The roots of colonialism were based on the implicit view that the lands (subjected to conquest) were being occupied by less evolved (inferior) peoples who were unworthy of occupying that land, therefore, justifying their exploitation and mistreatment.

Likewise, the anonymous contributor in Section 2 aptly titles their contribution 'Today as Yesterday' to show how White Saviors continue to irresponsibly invade Indigenous land and peoples under the guise of ethnotourism. They take away but don't give back. Similarly, Fernando David Márquez Duarte, in his piece on the American Non-Governmental Organization (NGO) Sea Shephard, whose unorthodox activities have already come under wide criticism, illustrates his anger and frustration at the deprivation of local Indigenous populations of their livelihoods under the misplaced guise of 'saving the fish'. Humans aren't the only thing White Saviors attempt to save, and green colonialism continues to impoverish Indigenous populations under similar premises. Duarte's piece is a cry from the heart about how White Saviorism chooses to annihilate rather than respect or work alongside.

Likewise, Rose Esther S. F. brings both Haiti's colonial past and its present subservience to international development interventions, showing how colonialism forcibly dispossessed the country of its Indigenous identity through White Saviorism. Slavery and colonization stole financial wealth and Indigenous knowledge from the land's original inhabitants to leave them in chains, both in the past as slaves and in the present as debtors to the international aid system. This desire to wipe out all that is Indigenous in the world is the crowning glory of White Saviorism. This echoes the colonial plunder of resources, both natural and human, that White populations seem to have an innate desire to control and, in the process, destroy.

DISTORTING PRACTICES OF DEVELOPMENT

The most critical aspects in implementing international development are modalities and methodologies. Modalities of how aid is to be disbursed and used and methodologies of how to control and manage these disbursements and their usage. These development 'practices', as they have come to be called, dominate the activities of international development and often reproduce White supremacy and the assumption of White benevolence.

Modalities of aid can easily hide activities that may not be part of traditional aid giving. As Robert Kakuru shows on the abuse of land rights in Central Uganda, multilateral organizations such as the World Bank work in tandem with corporate structures to create human displacement. The act of forced land grabbing is concealed under the guise of providing sustainable solutions to poverty. But the 'practice' of poverty alleviation–a wide-ranging objective of international development–actually creates more poverty, according to Kakuru, by replacing existing means of production with artificially generated practices such as vegetable oil production, reforestation and coffee plantations–all at the cost of human displacement and loss of livelihood.

Similarly, aid methodologies don't even bother to hide their disinterest in those they work with. As Sadaf Shallwani and Shama Dossa exhibit, the practice of development evaluation continues to perpetuate the White gaze of the savior. The success or failure of any development intervention by the Global North in the Global South can only be achieved using northern methods and northern human capital. The 'recipients' of those interventions cannot deduce whether they found the intervention helpful to their lives. Evaluation is only one methodology in the international development playbook that perpetuates Whiteness. Program design, objectives, country selection, and implementation mechanisms all emanate from the White Savior. These practices cannot be termed global, only Global North.

CREATING FALSE REALITIES

In his contribution, Kanakulya Dickson argues that similar to class-based false consciousness, White development practitioners often wrongly perceive their own practices. This leads to moral decadence and practical failure in the aid and development sector. The sense of obligation Rudyard Kipling talked about in his 1899 poem entitled 'The White Man's Burden' never led to equal relationships and moral actions. Using the title of Kipling's poem for his book on development failures, Easterly (2006) surprisingly never speaks of

'Whiteness', racism or racial divisions. Kanakulya palliates this by talking about development initiatives that are justified on moral terms but end up representing moral failure. Even the massacres of the religious crusades were justified under saviorism pretenses to save people from the 'wicked race' (Flaherty 2016, p. 14). Similarly, Christopher Columbus was justifying the genocide of the Americas to save the soul of non-Christians, despite developing an immoral system of exploitation, theft and dispossession.

From this, Michael George Kizito delves into the epistemological underpinnings of White Saviorism. He argues that humanitarian assistance and development practice are based on deep-seated 'inculcation of opinions, attitudes, perceptions, biases, distortions, disinformation and misinformation about development, poverty and wellbeing, right from childhood to adulthood'. In short, we are socialized into thinking of White people as saviors and Black and Brown ones as unable to save themselves.

THE WOMEN OF WHITE SAVIORISM

International development has a false assumption that the White Savior is male because, through a large part of its history, it has indeed been male dominated. As many of the contributions in this book detail, from the historical colonizers to present-day foreign donors and aid managers, it is primarily men who dominate and exert power and financial control in this world. But as Themrise Khan details in her chapter, White women have been as active, albeit less visible, players in colonial history over their Brown and Black wards. They have used their roles as nurturing mothers to starving and lost souls, as they did during colonial rule, to turn themselves into matriarchs of development in present-day aid modalities. In both cases, the sense of superiority over non-White people remains common.

Benhadjoudja develops this further with the case of Afghanistan as the ultimate example of White Saviors saving Brown women (which can also extend to women in Africa and Latin America) from their evil Taliban oppressors. The image of war is perhaps the most powerful in terms of saviorism, given the military's role in the imagination of nation-states, especially in a war waged to save Brown women. A force determined to do anything to rid the world of enemies, be it the Taliban, Saddam Hussain, or in more recent times, Vladimir Putin. And in the process, elevate those they oppress out of the depths of despair.

The language used above is not simply for the sake of literary flourish. It is how situations are described when it comes to the development of women in the Global South by the Global North. But what both Khan and Benhadjoudja allude to in their writing in differing contexts is that White women saviors are perhaps more dangerous than White male saviors due to their subjugation in their home countries. The issue of gender inequality is not limited to the Global South. As so much data, analysis, and lived experience have shown, White women are equally prone to inequality in White contexts. Thus, the opportunity to save women who are far less equal to them in other countries is an opportunity to exert the control they feel they lack elsewhere.

But the most significant finding in this area is that White Saviorism is gender-neutral. It is not necessitated on sex, but rather on the state of control that White peoples bring to the savior role and narrative. The operative word here is White. Therefore, to unpack saviorism, one needs to look at Whiteness through the eyes of all genders, as they manifest themselves in different ways.

THE WHITENESS OF BROWN SAVIORISM

While many forms of White Saviorism exist (see box on typology in the Introduction), White Saviorism is not only about White people (of all genders). Whiteness may appear to limit the moral wrongs within White Saviorism to White people alone, ignoring the possibility of 'Black' and 'Brown' individuals being agents of White Saviorism themselves. White Saviorism is not based on individuals with a certain skin colour being 'bad' and others being 'good', but on sustaining a social hierarchy based on race. In this field, as Themrise Khan explains in her chapter in this volume, racism 'comes from anyone associated with northern agencies–White, Black or Brown those who consider themselves marginalized in the North are as much the power brokers in the south as their White counterparts' (Khan 2021, see also Khan, this volume). Brown and Black people can also sustain Whiteness by attributing superiority to White ones or historically White countries. Heron (2007) uses the term 'bourgeois' to emphasize that Whiteness refers to a class, whereas others have used Western or Global North countries or people (Sondarjee 2020, Khan 2021).

Brown saviors, as identified in the contributions in Section 2 by Anonymous and Radha Shah, respectively, demonstrate how White Saviorism isn't just a physical manifestation in the guise of a White European but also a psychological manifestation in the minds of those who consider themselves superior to others, regardless of race or color. They, too, support White supremacy in the field of development. The story of the Brown representatives of a White international development institution acting precisely like their White counterpart in Bangladesh is an apt illustration of the influence the ethos of White Saviorism has on everyone it encounters. Everyone wants to be White, even if they are not, simply because of the power of Whiteness –even if they have to wield that power over their own.

Shah invokes this by presenting the interplay between Brown women in Pakistan on two different levels–the Brown Pakistani woman who represents her White donors more than her own country, and the Brown Pakistani woman whose origins are Pakistani but who is trapped between trying to be loyal to both her own Brown colleagues, as well as to the task at hand. Once again, the idea emerging from these stories (inspired by lived experiences) is that White Saviorism can seep into every crevice it can find. And the fact it seeps into the mindsets of those that it seeks to save is perhaps the most dangerous of all.

STEALING POWER THROUGH WHITE ORGANIZATION

Organizations and institutions have played the most far-reaching role in propping up the White Savior mindset because their very objective and ethos depend upon it. International development organizations exist because they only feel they can identify and fill in 'gaps' in countries less privileged than them. It is their employees who are then the messengers of this ethos. White Saviorism is thus a power structure but is lived in the daily lived experiences of Global South development practitioners today.

As both Jody-Ann Anderson and Chongo Beverly Anne Mwila show us through their lived experiences of working for such organizations in the Caribbean and Africa, respectively, the acceptance of anyone other than White is not considered to be of much importance other than filling in human resources gaps. And as Anderson suggests, filling them cheaply given the pay discrepancies between White and non-White. Amjad Mohamed Saleem also alludes to this in his experience as a

Brown Muslim humanitarian aid worker after the Sri Lanka tsunami. Locals perceive him as a White Savior riding his SUVs into disaster zones, as someone who must prove their worth to the cause, the 'cause' being decided upon not by nature but by how their specific organization views it. Eddy Michel Yao, on the other hand, looks into an often overused but understudied area of White voluntourism in development and how White, Western organizations use the Global South as training grounds for young minds to continue to perpetuate the imbalances of power.

All four authors narrate cases where the White organization makes the rules of engagement and disallows its followers to deviate from them. It is the sense of a formal organizational structure allowing the White Savior to justify its engagement and regulations over and above those it controls. But as Shah, Khan, Shallwani, Dossa and others demonstrate, Whiteness is often percolated into non-White minds through processes of internalization of sub-alternity (Saïd 1979).

BEING NON-WHITE IN A WORLD OF MANY COLORS

A cross-cutting theme that emerges across the majority of the contributions in this book is how White Saviorism impacts those non-White development practitioners who have grown up in White countries. A by-product of global migration, many grew up or moved to White Western nations, which they now call home but continue to see themselves as representatives of their non-White homelands. The international development industry is the perfect opportunity for many of these practitioners and scholars to both 'give back' to their homelands, as well as remain connected to their histories.

However, as authors such as Shallwani and Dossa, Anderson, Saleem, Yao and Shah have shown, being an expatriate non-White is not as simple as it sounds. The

241

boundaries of racism remain to hold them back down because of their skin color. One can see the north as one's homeland, but the north refuses to see them as populating the home. Therefore, initiatives to address systemic racism within Global North development sectors are welcomed but are not enough for the struggle against White Saviorism.

These migration processes impact native Global South inhabitants' dynamics with saviors of all hues. For many, it does not matter if the savior is or at least was one of their own. They represent a culture and state that sees them as inferior and whose institutions, now working in their countries, tend to perpetuate. The identity of the White Savior is forever enshrined in the identity of the nation it comes from, not necessarily that just the White color represents it. As explained in the introduction of this book by Teju Cole and other observers, White Saviorism is a complex structure of power, not only individually held attitudes and narratives.

WHAT NEXT?

This book has not set out to solve the dilemmas of White Saviorism. A single (or even many) book cannot achieve such a thunderous undertaking. But this book, and others like it, can ensure that White Saviors do not get off easily for their actions. And that their actions are documented and critically studied. We aimed to participate in a conversation that is ongoing, albeit not enough in academic circles and Western development agencies.

The contributions in this book have clearly articulated the many woes of the international development industry: its racist tendencies, its colonial attitudes, its lack of accountability, its lack of respect for its subjects, the lack of inclusion of those it works with and its attitude of superiority over others. White Saviorism is the vehicle through which these woes are translated and communicated on the ground. We often participate in a system of devaluing Black and Brown agency and worth.

Facing such dire observations about the state of the field, is it even possible to establish equal relationships between the Global North and Global South? Is it possible to dismantle an industry that lives off the 'underdevelopment' of others, whose 'bread and butter' are the continuing international inequalities (Manji and O'Coill 2002, p. 582). Cole (2012) asked, over a decade ago, how a 'well-meaning' Westerner can 'help' the Global South today: 'It begins, I believe, with some humility about the people in those places. It begins with some respect for the agency of the people of the Global South'. This means coming to terms with systemic racism in the field, not only its most visible instantiations, like lack of diversity in NGO boards but its racist foundations (Khan 2021). Only through such a process will we be able to develop true practices of solidarity among people.

As editors of this book, we have been critical of the global development project and the possibilities to reform it in our academic work and activism (Khan 2021, Dickson 2021, Sondarjee 2020). The contributors in this book reflect this postulate, from criticizing empowerment projects to environment protection to finance, mining and evaluation practices. 'While it is unclear at present how far development can exist in a deracialized form, what is deducible is that it is only through challenging racism within discourse and practice that its effects can be ameliorated to the benefit of the designated but occluded, "beneficiaries"' (Kothari 2006, p. 22). We believe Western countries and organizations need to recognize their role in the perpetuation of exploitation and devaluation of Global South communities. Still, we are uncertain of where this realization can lead.

REFERENCES

Cole, T. (2012) 'The White Savior industrial complex', *The Atlantic*, 21 March

Easterly, W. (2006) *The White Man's Burden: Why the West's Efforts to Aid the Rest Have done So Much Ill and So Little Good*, New York, Penguin Press

Flaherty, J. (2016) *No More Heroes. Grassroots Challenges to the Savior Mentality*, Chico, CA, AK Press

Kanakulya, D. (2021) *Pan Africanism, No White Savior Podcast*, https://podcasts.apple.com/us/podcast/pan-africanism-part-1-i-w-dr-kanakulya-dickson/id1499549147?i=1000467991935, accessed 15 August 2022

Khan, T. (2021) 'Racism doesn't just exist within aid. It's the structure the sector is built on', *The Guardian*, 31 August 2021, https://www.theguardian.com/global-development/2021/aug/31/racism-doesnt-just-exist-within-aid-its-the-structure-the-sector-is-built-on, accessed 15 August 2022

Kothari, U. (2006) 'An agenda for thinking about "race" in development', *Progress in Development Studies*, 6(1): 9-23

Heron, B. (2007) *Desire for Development: Whiteness, Gender, and the Helping Imperative*, Waterloo, ON, Wilfrid Laurier University Press

Manji, F. and Carl O'Coill (2002) 'The missionary position: NGOs and development in Africa', *International Affairs*, 78(3): 567-84

Mpangala, G.P. (2004) 'Origins of political conflicts and peace-building in the Great Lakes Region', paper presented at a Symposium Organized by the Command and Staff College (theme: 'Ramifications of Instability in the Great Lakes Zones'), Arusha, https://repositories.lib.utexas.edu/bitstream/handle/2152/5727/3000.pdf, accessed 15 August 2022

Saïd, E. (1979) *Orientalism*, New York, Vintage Books

Sondarjee, M. (2020) P*erdre Le Sud. Décoloniser La Solidarité Internationale,* Montréal, Écosociété

Appendix

About the Contributors

Jody-Ann ANDERSON is a Ph.D. candidate at the School of International Development and Global Studies at the University of Ottawa. Her research focuses on how institutions, like the police, can sustainably transform in contexts of increasing complexity. She has worked and currently works on various issues that include, but are not limited to, youth development, violence reduction, disaster risk reduction / climate change, White Saviorism, policing and security sector reform. She maintains hope for a peaceful and just world where all people, regardless of race, gender, citizenship, etc., can realize their full potential.

Leila BENHADJOUDJA is an anti-racism feminist and holds a doctorate degree in Sociology. Her research focuses on racism and anti-racism in Quebec, and her main publications focus on Islamophobia and Muslim feminism. She is the co-founder of the Feminist Festival in Ottawa and works as a professor at the Institute of Feminist and Gender Studies at the University of Ottawa.

Shama DOSSA is Manager Learning and Evaluation at Fenomenal Funds, a Feminist Funding Mechanism and associate professor in Social Development and Policy at Habib University, Karachi, Pakistan. She is a community development practitioner, researcher and academic with a specific interest in gender, disaster, reproductive health and rights in the Asia-Pacific region. Her work explores the link between theory and practice, drawing on arts-based and participatory methodologies. She is currently the Chair of the

Board for Shirkat Gah Women's Resource Centre, one of Pakistan's oldest feminist organizations.

Fernando David Márquez DUARTE is a Mexican decolonial activist and thinker from the Abya Yala. He has a B.A. in International Relations with an Honorific Mention from UABC and an M.Sc. in Regional Development from El Colegio de la Frontera Norte (COLEF) with a CONACYT scholarship. He is currently enrolled in the Ph.D. Political Science program at the University of California Riverside (UCR) with a Fulbright García Robles scholarship and the Dean's Fellowship. He has more than five years of teaching experience in different universities in México and the USA. Currently, he teaches at UCR. He has academic articles published in indexed journals of México, Brazil, Ecuador, Russia, Germany and the UK, and book chapters in México and Spain. He has advised and supported Indigenous groups such as the Triquis and Cucapáh Indigenous communities in Baja, California, México regarding Indigenous rights and political participation. He has also worked with the resistance in the defence of water in Baja, California, with a participatory action-research project. He is proficient in Spanish, English, Portuguese and Náhuatl languages.

Kizito Michael GEORGE is a lecturer in the Department of Religious Studies and Philosophy at Kyambogo University. He holds a Master of Philosophy degree in gender and development from the University of Bergen (Norway) and obtained a Ph.D. in development ethics from Makerere University in 2019. Dr. Kizito is a member of the American Philosophy Association (APA) and the International Development Ethics Association (IDEA). His research interests include development ethics, Pan-Africanism, White Saviorism,

247

human rights, poverty eradication, gender, jurisprudence and African philosophy.

Robert KAKURU is a lecturer of Human Rights in the Department of Philosophy, Makerere University, and holds a Ph.D. in Human Rights, a Master of Arts in Human Rights and a Bachelor of Development Studies. He has experience in lecturing / teaching, research and providing consultancy services. His core areas of teaching and research are natural resources and property rights, children's rights, international and regional human rights regimes, research methods, human rights monitoring, evaluation and reporting and theories of human rights. His consultancy engagements include policy research, strategic planning and management, program development, management, monitoring and evaluation, organization management, capacity-building and training, transparency and accountability, organizational capacity assessments, program evaluations, systems analysis and development, programming and organizational resource mobilization.

Kanakulya DICKSON is a lecturer at the College of Humanities and Social Sciences, Department of Philosophy, Makerere University. He holds a Ph.D. (Makerere, Uganda), Licentiate (Linköping, Sweden), M.A. Philosophy (Bergen, Norway) and B.A. (Makerere, Uganda). He has research interests in philosophy, ethics and governance. He has experience in collaborative research with national and international partners resulting in several publications. Dickson is co-editor of this volume.

Themrise KHAN is an independent development professional with over 25 years of experience in international development, gender, social policy and global migration. She has worked with several bilateral and multilateral agencies and international civil society organizations globally. Her main expertise lies in leading qualitative thematic and policy research studies and summative and formative evaluations of development programming. She has published both academically and as a research practitioner, including for the University of Ottawa Press and Routledge, as well as global think tanks and development agencies, on issues ranging from development aid intervention in fragile states to female labor migration. She is also a regular writer of op-eds and thematic pieces for various print and online mediums on development assistance, migration and gender. She has degrees from York University, Canada, and the London School of Economics and Political Science, UK. She is based in Pakistan. Themrise is co-editor of this volume.

Chongo Beverly Anne MWILA is an intersectional feminist and driven communication and advocacy professional who has been actively involved in interventions for the empowerment and advancement of women, children and young people since her mid-teens in the early 2000s. Since 2012, she has worked extensively on USG, USAID, United Nations systems and other donor-funded programming for girls' equitable access to education, advocacy efforts to increase all young people's (including those living with disabilities) access to relevant Sexual and Reproductive Health and Rights (SRHR) information and services, and capacity-building programs to reduce women's socio-economic vulnerability to sexual and gender-based violence (SGBV) and HIV. Chongo holds a bachelor's degree in communications from Simon Fraser University and began pursuing a master's degree in development studies from the University of Lusaka in 2021. Based in Lusaka, Zambia, she is currently juggling communications-based consultancies for clients around gender and SRHR.

Marcelo SAAVEDRA-VARGAS has been a political advisor to the vice presidency of the Confederation of Indigenous Nationalities of Ecuador (CONAIE), a representative in Canada of the Federation of Peasant Workers of the Department of La Paz-Tupaj Katari and president of the Peoples Support Group of the Americas (GAPA), Canada. He was a researcher for the North-South Institute (INS) and the Canadian Development Research Centre (IDRC), and a number of development-related non-government organizations (NGOs). He holds two bachelor's degrees: one in economics, specializing in economic development, and one in communication studies, specializing in mass media development. He also holds a master's degree in Diplomacy and a Ph.D. degree in International Relations from the Diplomatic Academy of Bolivia. He has been OPIRG leading elder and created the Indigenous Constitution exercise, anti(O)pression training, decolonization and indigenization workshops. He has been a professor at the University of Ottawa for the past 15 years and is currently teaching for the Institute of Indigenous Studies.

Amjad Mohamed SALEEM is a political scientist with extensive knowledge of peace-building, humanitarian affairs and development work. He has a particular interest in interfaith engagement and a focus on South Asia. He is currently focused his work on decolonization, anti-racism and dealing with diversity and inclusion within the multilateral sector. He has worked for different organizations on peace-building and humanitarian action. He is a regular contributor to different media posts and an alumnus of the International Visitors Leadership Programme and the Geneva Centre for

Security Policy. He has published in several journals, chapters in several books and published a book in 2008 entitled Lessons from Aceh. Amjad has an M.Eng. from Imperial College, London; an MBA from U21Global, Singapore; and a Ph.D. from Exeter University.

Radha SHAH is a social anthropological researcher with a background in south Asian studies who has worked for non-profits in Canada, Pakistan and Hong Kong. Her area of expertise spans rights advocacy for ethnic minorities, women, prisoners and migrant workers.

Sadaf SHALLWANI conducts and facilitates participatory research and knowledge generation from Global South perspectives in the areas of early childhood development, primary education, child rights and the effectiveness of grassroots civil society. Sadaf has two decades of research, evaluation and program development experience, including extensive work with different agencies of the Aga Khan Development Network in East Africa, South Asia and Central Asia. She has also designed and led several child development programs and research projects in Canada. Currently, Sadaf serves as Director of Learning and Evaluation at Firelight Foundation, where she plays a key role in the organization's efforts to shift power closer to community-based organizations and their communities in Sub-Saharan Africa, embrace and operationalize community-driven systems change and support communities to develop and carry out their own Indigenous and participatory approaches to evaluation and learning.

Rose Esther SINCIMAT FLEURANT has been a professor at the Université d'État d'Haïti (UEH) for more than 15 years. She completed her doctoral studies in social sciences at the UEH and holds a DEA in Gender, Population and Development. She completed her master's studies at the Faculty of Ethnology and has a degree in social communication. An expert / consultant in gender and local development, she has had a career in Haitian public administration. Committed to the fight for the respect of human rights, particularly women's rights, for over 25 years, she has been a facilitator / trainer and mobilization agent in education for responsible citizenship. She has provided technical support to numerous socio-community organizations, women's associations and youth associations in various municipalities of the Republic of Haiti. Former Director General of the Ministry of Women's Affairs and Women's Rights (MCFDF), she has also worked as a consultant and advisor on various technical and / or political issues in her expertise for local and international institutions. As a researcher in social sciences, she works on public policies, social movements (particularly women's movements), gender relations, population and local development.

Maïka SONDARJEE criticizes North / South inequalities from an anti-capitalist, anti-colonial and feminist viewpoint. She holds a Ph.D. from the University of Toronto, and she is an assistant professor at the School of International Development and Global Studies at the University of Ottawa. Her first book (Perdre le Sud. Décoloniser la Solidarité Internationale, 2020) was nominated for the Prix des Libraires du Québec. She is also a regular contributor for the Canadian newspaper Le Devoir. Maïka is co-editor of this volume.

Eddy Michel YAO is a candidate for the master's degree in International Development and Humanitarian Action Management at the Université Laval. He is originally from the Ivory Coast and is currently a volunteer project manager in

Senegal. He holds a bachelor's degree in Business Administration and a Graduate Diploma in Management from HEC, Montreal. He is particularly interested in north-south relations and African issues. He is at the service of communities in the south in order to build a more equitable world and develop their resilience in the face of crises situations.

FRONT COVER DESIGNER

Hikmatullah KHAROTI is a still and motion designer at Da Afghanistan Bank (Central Bank of Afghanistan) and holds an associate degree in graphic design. He was born in Helmand, Afghanistan. His recent works focus on digital payment and how to make Afghanistan cashless and free from fraud. He has given presentations to the President of Afghanistan, H.E. Ashraf Ghani, on TV Ads, motion videos, social media designs, print designs and narration. He was presented the creative designer award by H. E. Ajmal Ahmadi, governor of Central Bank of Afghanistan (DAB) and awarded the Future plan: 'To Make a World Where no one Become Someone' fellowship.